BRAND YOU

THESALONGUY'S
INSPIRATIONAL MEMOIR
TO TRANSFORM YOUR
LIFE AND BUSINESS

STEPHEN MARINARO

TESTIMONIALS

"Stephen's passion and work ethic have always been things that have caught my attention. Like many, he read Crush It. Like few, he executed."

—Gary Vaynerchuk

"The story of Stephen Marinaro and his rise to success is one of the most inspiring and intriguing stories out there. Stephen reveals the heartbreak of being an abandoned foster child, chronicles his insane days as a DJ in one of New York City's hottest venues, the Limelight, and unfolds his experience of becoming not only an entrepreneur, but one of the most sought after style and salon experts in America."

—Anthony Galie, Author,
Corporate Trainer, Keynote Speaker

"As they say, 'I knew him when,' and I'm glad to call him my friend as I am constantly astounded by his journey which has taken him to the Red Carpet at the Oscars, millions of viewers on YOUTUBE, and his own product line. For those who doubt that hard work and determination are no longer the ingredients for success and living out the American dream, pick up this book! You won't be disappointed!"

—Allan F. Wright, Author of eight books,
Adjunct Professor at Seton Hall University

FOREWORD

At the core of who he is and what he is all about, Stephen is a fun-loving guy with old-fashioned business values reminiscent of the Industrial Revolution-era New York City where all you needed was a dollar and a dream. As readers will quickly discover, Stephen's New York City demanded much more than that. In his world, hard work and relentless passion are the keys to success. His work ethic blends with unwavering compassion for people around him. His experience with adversity is his greatest source of strength in business.

What happens when a scared little boy gets taken in by a wonderful family and never loses that wild streak? Part genius, part madman, Stephen Marinaro paints a vivid picture of his epic journey through the highs and lows with this book. He takes the reader by the hand through what it feels like to be in the front—and back— of a police car as a police academy graduate, recovering bad boy, and bounty hunter. If you learn nothing else from this book, you will discover that bounty hunters in NYC always seem to get attacked by neighborhood dogs. In all seriousness, the book is not a step-by-step procedure that readers can follow to replicate success. Stephen is too smart to try to reduce his life path to something like that. Instead, he illustrates his values like constellations in the sky on a wild journey around the world without a map. His stark approach to storytelling shows readers what values helped and impeded his success in the greatest journey of all: the quest to unlock his true passion personally and develop himself professionally. Don't let the old world values fool you; the same values are his stars in the sky as he navigates two Internet technology bubbles to leverage his evolving, visionary brand.

When looking at Stephen's success on paper, it is easy to think it came naturally to a guy like him. This book shows you that the complete opposite is true. Stephen battled life's most frightening challenges by rolling up his sleeves and jumping out of the metaphoric airplane. In another world, Stephen would be the kind of guy that would jump off a mountaintop with a sword in hand to land on a flying dragon, tame it mid-flight, and ride the beast to victory. In the world of this book, Stephen has both feet firmly grounded in the reality of his humble situation and learns what it takes to bring his business visions to fruition. This hard-working guy from New Jersey meets challenges at the risk of peril for a mere chance at life's greatest reward—earning his place as the runt of his foster family and proving that his business visions are not too progressive.

Readers see that in business and life, Stephen is still that abandoned foster child scared out of his mind to tell the judge whom he wants his real mother to be. His stories reveal the grown-up version of that frightened boy, chronicling his encounters with Hollywood's elite and the business world's most sought-after multimillionaires. What will this star-struck boy from New Jersey discover about business? What does family mean to this foster child? What is his true identity? In this rocket-ship ride to the stars and back, it is a pleasure to read Stephen's experiences in an artful, logical composition. I can't wait to join readers in sharing this wild ride. Stephen takes us by the hand for a once-in-a-lifetime, all-access adventure where dreams—and nightmares—come true.

—Benjamin J. Theisen, Entrepreneur, Author, Mental Health Expert

P.S. Whenever I think of Stephen, the power suit is the first thing that comes to mind. It's hilarious to see him in Los Angeles and perhaps someday you will get the chance. I don't know what they do in Jersey, but can anyone help me convince Stephen we don't wear business suits to breakfast diners in LA? (Just joking, buddy. You know I love you like a brother.)

PREFACE

For over 35 years, I have been a public speaker, trainer, and business coach. As such, I've worked with people at nearly every level of business from CEOs to trainees. As would be expected, most of the individuals I've worked with were "average" in terms of drive, skills, motivation, work ethic, etc. My job was to help them break through their own mental barriers and reach a fuller potential. Unfortunately, many were unfocused, unable, or unwilling to accept and adopt new strategies that would help them get to where they claimed they wanted to be. One of the great frustrations in my business is knowing that the person you are working with is capable of so much more, yet watching them continue to limit themselves and self-sabotage their careers. They are, as we say in the business, "uncoachable." However, after a while, you tend to develop a feel for who is going to move forward, and who is likely to remain fixed in their mindset.

A few years ago, I was working in my garage after hours when the phone rang and I answered it. The young man on the other end introduced himself as Stephen Marinaro. He explained that he had stumbled on some videos I had posted on YouTube and found them to be very interesting. After describing what he did, he wanted to know if he could ask me a few questions about goal setting, focus, and mindset. I told him that

I was fixing a broken generator, but if he didn't mind me working while talking to him, he could fire away. He proceeded to ask some very specific questions about how to reach the next level in his career as he had a plan and was determined to implement it. The fact that he had such a clear-cut career strategy was the first thing that caught my attention (most people don't). And as he asked his questions, it soon became obvious that I was dealing with a man who was going places.

I answered his questions and described a few techniques to him that would help him to make adjustments and changes in his mindset that would likely result in an increase in his productivity. As the conversation ended, he asked if he could call me back after he had implemented the changes so that we could evaluate the results. I agreed with one caveat—that he not call until he had at least tried the techniques we had discussed and could report the results. Knowing how difficult it is for most people to accept advice and change their habitual ways of doing things, I hung up, never expecting to hear from him again.

But sure enough, a few weeks later he called back with a detailed description of the changes he had made and the results to date. He asked what the next step was. That was the moment I knew I had stumbled on to the rarest of things in the business world—someone who knew exactly where he was going and was willing to do what it took, no matter how difficult, to get there. There is an old statement in the world of motivational speaking (no sexism intended): "You can't beat a man with a plan."

Stephen and I do not speak often, as we are both very busy people. As I follow his career on Social Media and the Internet, I have watched with fascination and awe as he has built a large and thriving business that has no limits. He is well on his way to realizing and even exceeding his dreams. No one has worked harder or deserves it more. It would be nice to take some credit for his success but that is simply not the case. Stephen was smart enough to seek out and consult with many mentors, taking the best from each and creating his own formula for success. He did it. The student has become the master.

As you read this book and realize how many obstacles were placed in his path throughout his life, you begin to realize the magnitude of his accomplishment. But then you also realize that if you have a clear, detailed vision, and are willing to work hard to achieve it, literally anything is possible. Stephen Marinaro is the American Dream personified.

—Anthony Galie
Author, Corporate Trainer, Keynote Speaker

INTRODUCTION

Ready to change your life? Looking for a new outlook and a fresh perspective—a bright, new way to look at the world? Read on....

I wrote Brand You to give you an inspiring wake-up call—a brand new or "Brand You" way to look at the world with a refreshing vision of how to conduct business, live your best life, and seize control over any situation simply by being you. Why am I the expert? My life's journey has been full of some positive and negative experiences that have taught me many powerful lessons. I stared death in the face, took on challenges most people would avoid, experienced tremendous loss when my mother passed away in my arms, and lived a life full of risks and rewards.

What I am going to share with you in this book will shock, inspire, motivate, and give you a new perspective on your life. As I walk you through my journey, you will see that my life has been full of adversity and obstacles. I was born into an unstable family, put up for adoption, did unusual things like hunt for fugitives, and had a lot of incredible experiences in-between. I promise my story will create a new outlook on how you can take control of any situation from business to your personal life.

We live in a world of challenges, obstacles, and the need to adapt to any given situation. I have found that the only way to learn how to survive is to go through life's troubles and experiences. I have felt the pain that drove me to reach for success, faced the fear that motivated me to not give up, and tackled the tasks of making opportunities happen.

As I experienced in so many situations, I wanted to help inspire other people to do things differently. So I decided to write Brand You. If you feel lost, are in need of inspiration, or a source of motivation, my experiences will show you how to overcome adversity to survive, and even thrive. Applying the skills and outlooks I have learned through my training, education, and hard work will help you discover a new perspective to apply to your life or profession. I am not suggesting you duplicate my life experiences. Instead, I want you to learn from them and think about how you might adapt them to your own life to succeed.

One of the ways I am going to teach you is through ideas to build a personal brand. Personal branding has emerged from self-help management techniques. The personal brand concept suggests that success comes from self-packaging and marketing. I seemed to be an innate natural at creating a personal brand. I started building a brand for myself without even knowing it since I was 12 years old. Making people laugh and putting on performances was something normal for me in school. Little did I know that putting myself in front of an audience would later become the main core of how I do business, and in essence, how I built my brand.

Brand You will describe how to build your personal brand. Then you can envision anything that you want to do in life. We all need a source to inspire and motivate us. I now invite you into my world for the next 100 pages or so. I also want to thank you for your interest in my story.

—Stephen Marinaro, *TheSalonGuy*

CHAPTER 1

CHILDHOOD

I WAS BORN INTO THIS WORLD SHORTLY AFTER MY FATHER SHOT himself in the head on the front lawn. It was my mother's dream to have a son after having four girls. I learned this when I was about 10 years old, but we will get into this subject later in the book. There are still speculations and many unanswered questions when it comes to my biological parents. Because of my father taking his own life, my mother became very unstable and a rebel. This situation led to her neglecting me and not being able to properly care for me. From what I learned, some of the conditions she put me in were so bad that people had to call the police to take me out of them. I recall one to this day, which was being left in the car as a baby. Not just for a few minutes, but hours. The police came to question my mother and basically saved me from what would have been a very hard and troubled life.

I was taken to a foster home where I ended up under the care of Josephine Marinaro. She was a foster mother who had taken care of over 80 children—many of whom would sometimes leave after a few days. I was told that I was a cute baby (platinum blonde curls and blue eyes). My hair is long gone, but I still have those blue eyes. Josephine, my foster mom, could not let me go. She took it upon herself to adopt me. Believe me when I say that adoption back in the 1970s was much different than it is today. It took her almost six years to adopt me. The court system issued a long, drawn-out investigation, which still occasionally put me under my mother's care. Josephine cared for me on a part-time basis.

I still cannot remember why the time was split up between them. There is not a whole lot that I can remember about my birth mother except that she had long, brown hair. I was in the backseat one time and I recall her driving. Some guy was in the passenger seat. He asked me where I wanted to go. I wanted to go to a local amusement park. I think I was about age 4 or 5. Another haunting moment was when I was taken to a large, blue building. I did not know what that was back then, but I always cried in terror when I saw it. Turns out it was the county building that dealt with adoptions and other cases. It was a very loud, busy, and scary environment for me. Those two things were all I could honestly remember from my first four to five years.

I also recall the exact day I had to go into court to decide who was going to be my mother. I was in second grade and was all dressed up in a suit and bow tie. Everyone in the class was confused as to where I was going. I said to go to be with my mom and get my name changed. I do not remember a lot from the actual court session except being taken into the judge's chambers. He asked whom did I want to live with. Now before I share my answer, I want to give you some perspective on it. Josephine kept a diary of my visits with her and her journey during my adoption. It was very hard to read it, so I read it when I was much older. She would note things like: "Stephen was very quiet today. He seemed very sad and just not his happy, normal self." "Stephen was in a very good mood today and wouldn't stop smiling." "Stephen cried all day and something seemed very off." The different moods and conditions I was in varied from visit to visit. From these journal entries, it was obvious I was living in an unhealthy environment; however, I just cannot remember what went on.

So let's go back to whom I chose. The judge asked me whom I wanted to live with, and I pointed to Josephine. I said, "Her." The judge then ordered that Josephine was going to be my adopted mother and my name changed from Steven DeWoolf to Stephen Andrew Marinaro. Thus, I had carried the name DeWoolf till second grade. It was definitely a transition getting adjusted to my new last name, but this was now my family and a new life lay ahead of me.

Josephine, who I will refer to as my mother from now on, adopted me as a widow. She was also mother to my two sisters, Carmelyn and Mary Lu, and my brother, Pat. Mother was in her fifties when she adopted me so everyone in the family is much older than I am. People used to think that my sisters or brother were my parents, which used to make me mad.

Mother watched children for a living. She was pretty much a saint and was loved by many. Everyone called her by the name Aunt Jo. She was a tiny Italian woman, but she was as tough as General Patton. I do recall shortly after the adoption became official, my biological mom broke into the new house where I was living and grabbed me.

"She's not your mother!" my biological mom declared. "I am— and I always will be!"

Mother got to her and immediately ushered out of the house— and that literally was the last time I saw my biological mother. She is still alive and can easily be reached; however, it is still a very tough topic and situation for me. As an adult, I still have haunting memories and feel fearful to meet her. I keep in touch with one of my biological sisters named Kim from time to time. She shared much of my biological mother's side of the story—after all, there are always two sides to every story.

My adoption definitely had a huge impact on certain aspects of my life. Psychologists commonly say that your childhood, especially before the age of 8, builds the foundation for how you see the world in your adulthood. According to Ann Smith in the article, "Can Our Childhood Really Predict Our Future," that was published by *Psychology Today*, "I am not a believer in the 'blame-the-parents' approach to life. I do believe that our childhood experiences, which include parents, combined with our own personalities, our reaction to siblings and peers, and the context of our lives send us off on a path with a particular set of beliefs and patterns that have a huge impact on our future relationships."

I agree. Many people have childhood stories or memories that continue to affect their decision-making, choices of relationships, or emotional reactions to situations. It applies to me, especially in my choices of women that often reflect how Mother treated me. I know! Who the hell wants that? Yet relationships in particular are heavily influenced by childhood experiences and behavior modeled to you by the adults in your life. There is not a day that goes by where I do not think of my first six years, and even things that randomly pop up in my head. I could still meet my biological mother and maybe that would close some doors, but I still have not done it.

Many of my adult issues stem from my adoption. Sometimes the differences between you and your adopted family are so wide that as you grow older, these problems become even bigger—and can even cause depression. We all have our own personalities, characteristics, traits, attitudes, and gifts that make us unique and special. For me, as an adopted son, something about our differences seemed dramatically enhanced to me.

Don't get me wrong. My family was very good to me. They gave me a great life. They rescued me from what could have been a tough, stressful, and unstable upbringing. I am grateful that I was looked after so well my whole life. Yet this does not imply we blended as one happy family without problems. As I just said, I am very different from my adopted family. They all have similar traits and genetic connections while I do not share those things.

Being adopted comes with many feelings and emotions that biological children often do not understand. As a result of inherent differences often based on biology, children of adoption sometimes experience feelings of detachment when it comes to their adopted families. I know that I at times felt strong feelings of detachment when it came to certain aspects about how I viewed life versus my family's views and considerable differences in our personalities.

One of my biggest problems related to being adopted are my feelings of abandonment. After doing some research I learned those feelings are normal for adopted people. You just have to see it through my perspective: The one woman who was supposed to love and care for me was either sometimes around or running off, which led me to feeling abandoned and confused. Then came this other woman who was there for me and ended up adopting me, but she did not give birth to me. You cannot take away that connection a child has with his or her mother.

Despite any issues, I feel blessed to have grown up the way I did. The Marinaros are a hard-working Italian family. I was raised in an upscale, healthy, stable environment, but it was not without its drama. Yes, it was very interesting, and there was more drama than a reality TV show. The food, functions, funerals, and weddings were pretty much where we all saw each other (if you are Italian, you know exactly what I am talking about). I have so many fond memories of my family, cousins, and people I would see at family functions that always treated me as one of their own. Not everyone knows of my adoption. Here is the interesting thing about being from an Italian family. The connections are astounding. I can meet someone and somehow find out he or she is my cousin. I sometimes run into cousins I have not seen in 15 years or long-lost cousins I have never met. Funerals and weddings are great places to connect with these family members.

The best thing I learned from my adopted family was to have a strong work ethic. I learned about working and how sitting on your ass would get you nowhere in life. When I was old enough, Mother told me to get up and get a job. She encouraged me to keep active. As an adopted Italian son, I learned that you always work and have something you can do to earn money. As the old cliché goes, "Money doesn't grow on trees." Our family taught me not to sit around and wait for money to just show up—or well, you would be waiting a very long time.

You might be wondering what happened to Mother's husband. His name was Larry and he passed away before I was born. I literally grew up fatherless. I had some father figures in my life such as my brother-in-law, Frank, my brother, Pat and my friends' fathers growing up. I always felt uncomfortable when kids used to ask me about my dad or when fathers were brought up in school. I would just sit there thinking to myself that I had no dad, and I did not know what it was like.

My childhood made me into who I am today. The circumstances around it shaped me. As a result, I am somewhat of a loner. Since I could not rely on the woman who gave birth to me, I became self-reliant. Then the disconnections between my adopted family and me contributed even more to this pattern of self-reliance (later in the book I will share how this self-reliance applies to my current life and business).

Regardless of anything else, my adopted family has been there for me through thick and thin. They have supported me as any family would support their own. Yet I still have a biological imperative to seek out blood connections. As I grew up and faced the aftermath of my rocky beginnings, adoption and blending into my new family, I began to feel long-repressed emotions. The feelings from early childhood started to catch up with me. I started to view my life through a different perspective—and it changed the way I thought and felt about life.

As I grew older, I wanted to learn as much as I could about my biological family. I really only had one person who was blood-related and that was my sister, Kim. She was the youngest out of the four girls and was the one closest to me in age. She was always looking out for me when she could and formed a bond with me during the short time we had together. I met up with her when I became an adult. It felt uncomfortable, yet it was also refreshing to connect with a real, blood-related sibling.

I also discovered my biological heritage. I am part Italian and half German, or that is what I thought for my whole life. Talking with Kim, I learned that I have some Belgian, French, and Dutch in my bloodline as well. My biological father was from Europe and my mother was Italian. We look a lot alike actually, and you can totally see the resemblance to my biological family.

When she shared her side of the story, it confused me even more. My adopted family had told me my mother got into trouble, but some of the information conflicted with what my sister said. The conflicting details mystify me. So I can only believe what seems realistic about it.

Despite what I have been told, I am not 100 percent sure of my early years and pre-adoption experiences.

I do know my father took his life. I used to question why he would do such a thing with four daughters and a baby on the way, but I was told that he felt guilty for all the bad things he had been doing. Whatever was going on, he had felt it was not fair to his family. The house that contained all of the family's photos, documents, and memories had burned down. There was nothing left for me to see or even learn from. I have no idea what caused the fire. All I know is that in my 30s, I still had never seen what my father looked like. I have no clue except I was told he was very handsome.

Shortly after that revelation, I received a letter in the mail from Kim that contained two pictures. There he was—for the first time in my life, I saw my father! He looked like James Dean: blonde hair, chiseled cheeks, and super handsome. I got a rush of joy for not only being proud he was my dad, but this marked a huge step for me in my life. I finally knew what he looked like. I actually put the pictures in a special place and can look at them anytime I want.

I wanted to start the book with my childhood experiences to help you understand and get to know *me*. I was spoiled my whole life. I am super thankful to my family for such great care and love, but those first 5–7 years were a journey and book in and of itself. Those years taught me to feel normal about being alone and experience a disconnection with family and even society. It really affected me as an adult, and to this day still has an impact on me. There is not a day that goes by where I do not think about my adoption in some capacity.

Most of my role models and mentors all have stories and built their success from either a major tragedy in their lives or hitting rock bottom. I will get into my tragedy and how it fueled my business later into the book. Now, I would like to share my schooling and teen years and how those years impacted my life.

CHAPTER 2

MY FORMAL AND LIFE EDUCATION

I WENT TO CATHOLIC SCHOOL PRETTY MUCH THE WHOLE TIME during my childhood and teenage years. My family attended Catholic school, too. If you went to Catholic School back in the day, you are probably aware of the abuse students sometimes endured. By today's standards, it is considered abuse, but back then it was normal.

Nuns back then were allowed to hit and chase you around for doing something wrong. Because the school system was private and exclusive, it was like being locked away in prison—and whatever happened in there stayed in there.

My class was very small and had more girls than boys. I can recall going to pre-school and adjusting to being around other kids. Most of my grammar school years were spent with the same classmates till graduation. I was, and still am, a jokester. If you know me, you know I love to make people laugh. I was voted class clown every year in school. From putting on skits to doing stand-up routines, comedy was something I always loved even as a kid.

The stories are endless when it came to being under the supervision of nuns. They were like the gatekeepers to heaven. Trying to get educated while at the same time learning about Catholicism was a lot for me. Stories about devils to seeing miracles were a normal part of discussions during school. Imagine going home to share that Sister Mary saw a demon in her room. Regardless of the various topics, we got a good education and formed strong bonds in school. I have reconnected with some of my classmates, and it was great to talk about our memories.

I had a childhood best friend named Rodney who lived down the street from me. We used to ride our bikes together to school in all weather conditions. From rainstorms to 10-degree weather that caused us to grow icicles on our eyebrows by the time we got to school. We would run to the radiator just to defrost. It then became a tradition to go over to the grandmother's house of our classmate named Kenny every day after school. We would do the most dangerous, unsafe, and ridiculous activities from a game called "mud ball" (covering a Nerf football in mud and throwing it at a person as he climbed up a tree) to completely eating all the food in the pantry.

We may have been educated in a strict Catholic school, but it did not stop us from turning into rebels and doing some really stupid things. We also had a friend named Carlos. The two of us were the equivalent of the adult cartoon *Beavis & Butthead*—only on speed. Matthew and Mike were some great guys too. We played sports, went fishing, and enjoyed fun outdoor activities. I also cannot forget girls like Stephanie who was my girlfriend for a day or proposing to Chrissy in second grade. We were all very close when we were young. I have so many wonderful memories about my friends. I will never forget them as well as my classmates from St. Bart's.

School also had its tough times. I used to get teased and bullied because I had full lips, a big head, and I always chased girls around. The only thing that has changed is, well, nothing! As I just mentioned, I proposed to Chrissy and even gave her a ring. We set up a pretend wedding outside the church at school. It lasted a day I think.

A WORD ABOUT BULLIES

Since I mentioned the teasing and bullying, I want to discuss that subject a little more in-depth. I was personally bullied starting in grammar school. It went on throughout high school. Even later in life, I would meet the occasional "prick" who would make a smart comment. I pretty much ignore that sort of thing now. I feel proud that I do not disrespect people that way.

However, we live in a society where bullying has caused some people to take their own lives. It is something that can stay with you forever. I still have certain insecurities because I was made fun of in school. No matter how successful you are, how good looking, or how much money you make, bullying can have long-term emotional affects. If you were bullied, it sticks with you. Bullies' words and actions can soak right into your soul. When you grow up, the ridicule and comments can also affect how you make business decisions, find the right relationships or create a healthy family. I have learned that you must overcome those thoughts and insecurities because they will drag you down and keep you there for a long time.

First, you need to understand the source and forgive those kids because they did not know any better and what they told you was not true. As for adults who can be assholes, they do not have that excuse so ignore them. Kids though are still learning manners, developing personalities, and managing feelings.

What misguided kids said to me no longer defines me. Instead of questioning compliments and nice words, I appreciate and accept them. As role models and parents, the best lesson we can teach our kids is that beauty comes from within.

One of the biggest things I have also learned through my younger-year experiences was that all those positive lessons about manners and how to treat other people was meant to prepare me to be a better adult. I still use the things I was taught when I deal with other people. I have adopted the motto, "Treat others the way you wish to be treated." Today, I apply that saying to how I run both my personal and business relationships. I am going to get super hardcore into the business side of things later in the book, but do you see how once again, your childhood can have a long-term impact? So do not let your negative experiences keep you down!

BACK TO GROWING UP

Realizing now how I was treated in school has affected me has given me great self-awareness about why I did the things I did. Now I understand why I put on all of those "performances" in school. I learned to make people laugh *with me* not at me. The bonus was that I made people laugh, entertained them, and brought them joy. I also did not realize it at the time, but I was building a brand for myself, building up my character and becoming comfortable around people. This is probably the most important lesson in life to this day that I apply in how I do business. I will get into this subject more in the business chapter.

I graduated 8th grade and decided to go a Catholic high school. My class was much larger, but we graduated with no more than 100 kids. I was kind of lost and nervous the first day of high school much like any person would be. I was just trying to remember to walk left from the main lobby after I got off the bus to get to my locker. I do not know how they expected us to get from one side of the school to another in like, four minutes. I hear schools are like that even now but with quadruple the number of students. Eight-hundred kids in one freshman class alone were expected to move that fast? That is just unheard of to me. High school was a *very* interesting time in my life. I experienced some of the scariest things to the most adventurous.

During most of my childhood and teen years, I made friends with a variety of nationalities and races. Pretty much 90 percent of my friends were not Caucasian. I learned so much about different cultures. Everyone's friends and families accepted me. Because of how I was raised, I was well mannered, polite, and very obedient. I would always listen and do what I was told. Even from an early age, I was taught about respect, which plays a huge role in how I do business and interact with people. My mother used to joke and ask me if I had any white friends. Now that I think about it, I did not! Back then, it was about people not race. I felt comfortable and was accepted. I just went with what seemed normal. From the way I dressed to the music I listened to. Also, music played a huge role in my life, and I will be sharing my experiences of DJing at 12 years old to going to the most controversial nightclubs in New York City.

Once I went to high school, I was exposed to so many different styles, groups, nationalities and probably five times the number of people. It was very intimidating. I got the hang of school and started to settle in. Making new friends, hanging with groups and really figuring out where I fit in. Each year I changed my style and the people I hung around. It seemed everyone changed the same way. We used to look forward to the first day of school to see who changed their style. Some stayed the same but many changed, including me. I went from thinking I was black to then Spanish to Filipino. It was all because I felt so comfortable around different people. It was not about race as much back then.

I was the token white kid with blonde hair and blue eyes. I definitely stood out, but was accepted by everyone. I will never forget the group of guys that I was pretty much closest with throughout high school, and that included Andy, Tito, Mario, and Mark. I was also acquainted with a lot of people, but those guys were the ones that I considered my closest buddies.

In my sophomore and junior years, I started hanging out with the wrong crowds. I got into trouble—serious trouble. One night in a park with a bunch of people I thought were my friends, I ended up taking the heat for someone else. I was the one taken in by the cops. It pained me when my mother and family had to come pick me up at the station very late at night.

However, that experience taught me something significant—something so important it helped turn my life around. As I sat in the backseat of the police car, I saw about 50-plus people all lined up against a wall cheering and waving to me. I felt cool for all of three seconds until I realized I did not know these people. It occurred to me here that I was taking the heat for another guy and getting cheered on for getting into trouble. I decided then and there that it was time to make a change.

Fortunately, the charges were dropped. The judge on the case realized I had gotten caught up in the wrong crowd and was at the wrong place. He encouraged me to stay away from those people. I heard him loud and clear. I immediately stopped hanging around them. I went cold turkey and cut them off. It was all for the best.

I got my life back on track and began to enjoy high school during my senior year. I continued to be the class clown. While I used to feel hurt when people made fun and laughed at me, I now realized I could make them laugh with me. I loved making people happy. It came natural to me and still does to this day. I do warn you that I may just dedicate a chapter to my bad jokes! From all the dances, formals, proms, cliques, friends, crazy experiences and everything that happened, I was starting to come into my own as a young man.

While I had been hanging out with the wrong people, I had maintained my long-time friends. I was fortunate to have friends like Rodney and his family. They treated me like I was their own son. They took me on camping trips, served me Filipino food, shared their culture, and invited me to family gatherings. It was a huge part of my life being around Rodney, his sister, Rachelle, and their parents. His Mother, Mrs. Canete, passed away in 2009. It was tough for everyone as is always the case when you lose a loved one.

It is really valuable to grow up around ethnically diverse families. You learn about other people's cultures and their differences. I would feel either jealous or thankful about my upbringing. Even as a kid, I thought it was fascinating what the parents of my friends did for a living, the foods they ate or the activities they enjoyed. I wanted to be like them when I got older.

When it came to education, I spent a lot of time in school. With all of the classes I took, I probably have the equivalent to a master's degree. When I graduated, I was a little uncertain about what I wanted to do with my life. My guidance counselor explained my grades were not good enough to get into the college I wanted to attend. So I took some time off and then got started with my career in the salon industry. Believe me though, I have tried my hand at many things.

I graduated high school and took some college courses. I also attended the fire science and police academies and got a 911 certification. I took classes in Hazmat operations, rescue operations, fugitive recovery operations and a bunch of ongoing educational classes in business and beauty. I know it seems all over the place and somewhat confusing, but it has made me the person I am today. The diverse nature of my education also instilled in me the ability to adapt to just about any situation in life and business.

The main reason I am sharing all of this with you is so you can get to know *me* as a person. I have achieved much of my success based on being transparent with who I am as a person and how I want to be remembered. There is still much more to learn about me, so be prepared to come along on this journey into my life and the experiences I have encountered. What we go through makes us who we are as people. We often need to go through many challenges to see clearly and find our path in life. Now, I invite you to keep reading the next few chapters where I am going to take you deeper into my life. As you read each one, I hope you begin to see the overall big picture and understand my message.

CHAPTER 3

NIGHTLIFE

TOOK AN INTEREST IN BEING A DJ WHEN I WAS ABOUT 13 YEARS old. I used to listen to rap radio stations and DJs that inspired me to start mixing tapes into records. I also grew up in a family where we all enjoyed music. My sister was a music teacher and played in a rock band. Another sister sang opera and my brother played the drums in high school. So my life was filled with listening to music, going to the theater, and enjoying all sorts of entertainment. By the time I started spinning records, it was a natural thing.

Let's move right to the exciting parts of this era. My stories are mind-blowing and I am lucky to be alive after all the crap I got myself into. I came of age right when the New York City nightclubs were the hottest places to be and what was going on in them was all over the news. The drugs, the Club Kids, the controversy, and all the excitement gave me a rush.

I began expanding my DJ career in high school and things really started to get interesting my senior year and after graduation. I was exposed to the club scene in NYC in the early 90s. When I say it was crazy, it was crazy. I was too young to have a Studio 54 experience, but this scene made up for it. The first time I set foot into a club in NYC, I felt so overwhelmed. I had been in clubs before but nothing ever like this one.

I remember my old friend Dennis joined me as we walked up to someone who was managing the rope guarding the entrance. Our sole objective was to get into this club, but I heard it was impossible. Rumor had it that it was mostly a gay club. Since we were both straight we hatched a scheme. We held hands and pretended we were gay to get in. We walked up to the door guy and he asked for our IDs. He also took a special liking in me and said I was cute. Man, that was awkward. We were both so nervous, but we got in.

We joyfully got into the club and felt ecstatic we had done it. The lights, music, energy, it was all in our faces. Distracted in our excitement, we had no idea of what to do next. We walked around in the areas the bouncers allowed us into. This nightclub was one of the most popular in NYC at the time. It was surreal, from the stripper cages to the people hooking up in the dark corners to the people doing drugs on tables right out in the open. I knew right then and there that I was hooked to this type of place.

That opened up my mind to what the other nightclubs were going to be like if they were all like this one. Since I was a DJ, I was interested in the DJ who was spinning that night. My business instincts kicked in. I immediately started thinking about how I could become a DJ in one of these clubs. I started talking to people and hearing about other nightclubs in NYC. I thought this was the prime spot, but apparently, this was just the beginning.

I saw groups of people that were clearly not normal in the way they dressed. They were flamboyant, unique, and very different. I saw people dressed like they were from outer space or wore insane things like six-inch shoes. Crazy hair, crazy outfits, crazy makeup—and I loved it. I ended up seeing these people out and about in NYC the more times I went back to this particular club and got to know everyone.

That night I ended up meeting and talking to one person from this clique called Club Kids. They basically ran the NYC nightlife. They were also referred to as "freaks." I decided to approach one of them, a guy by the name of Astro Earle. I went up to him because he fascinated me. The way he and all the others looked, dressed, danced—it was enticing. I did not want to be them, but I wanted to hang out with them.

So I approached Astro and told him I was a DJ. My goal was to sell myself to him and give him the idea I could DJ at one of these clubs. He responded by telling me to give him a tape and he would listen to it. His request immediately boosted my confidence. I felt so good about making him a tape. I knew I could absolutely crush it. This was a prime opportunity that presented itself—and it was essentially giving me an opener.

Right after I had made the tape but had not yet given it to Astro, I heard about another club called The Limelight—and many of my experiences would take place there. This nightclub was one of the biggest, most controversial nightclubs in NYC. So many documentaries have been made about The Limelight and its owner than any other I know. Clearly, this was harder to get into than the last club.

I somehow managed to get into the club and happened to run into Astro. I used the chance meeting to give him the tape that I had on me. I had no idea what to think, but I was confident he would like it. About a week later, he told me that he really enjoyed it. He then told me that he was running a party for all the Club Kids and that he wanted me to DJ at it. I was beyond blown away when I heard this invitation. I had found my way in—I had made it. Little did I know that this party started at 6:00 a.m. I prepared my records, grabbed a couple of friends, and told them about this opportunity and that it would be my best set ever.

So it was 6:00 a.m., and I got to this club. Turns out that it was not a club, but a bar in the middle of nowhere. Surprisingly, by 6:30 a.m., the place was packed with Club Kids and guests—everywhere. I swear, they were coming out of the floor!

It was so underground it was crazy. Within 10 minutes, people were approaching me, asking if I was from Amsterdam but I answered with smirks on my face saying I was from Jersey. Actually, most of my inspiration for sets came from Amsterdam's music scene so I can see the mistake. My average was 160 beats-per-minute, which is pretty damn fast if you are not familiar with music.

So I was playing my set and a guy came up to me and also asked me where I was from. I told him I was from Jersey like I did with everyone else, but this guy responded a little differently. He said he wanted me to come play at his party at a club he spun at. I found out he ran a party at The Limelight every Wednesday. It turns out this guy was one of the top DJs in NYC, a guy named Keoki. I had no idea who this guy was at the time and just said, "Okay cool, man."

The lesson here is to always take advantage of opportunities. Learn to say, "Yes!" The minute I took advantage of one opportunity, many good things started to happen.

Even as a young man, no matter what I was doing I was always trying to sell myself and do the best I could, and I have had so many positive outcomes from it.

After this guy told me about this party, I went home and thought it over. I decided to call him to set up a date for when I would DJ at the club. I had become friends with a guy named David who soon became a great friend and basically kept a look out for me, connected me with the right people, and acted like my guardian. I called Keoki from David's house.

Keoki told me I could DJ on a particular night, but I would have to sleep with him in order to get this chance. At the time, I had a girlfriend, plus I was straight. I was very angry about his request. I said that I do not sleep with people to get gigs. I stood my ground and instead of rejection, I obtained his respect. He said, "Well, come this night and that'll be the night you can DJ." The lesson here is to always hold your integrity no matter what is at stake.

I was super excited about this. I told all my friends. He wanted me to DJ Thanksgiving eve of all nights. For you non-club goers, the eve of Thanksgiving happens to be the biggest night for nightclubs— and that was going to be my night to DJ! I put together a guest list of all my friends, which was a solid 20 people. I remember going to the front entrance of The Limelight and the people had to go check that I was actually DJing there.

I handed over my guest list. Then I walked into the largest monster party I had ever seen in my life. The club was actually an old church converted into a nightclub. Stained-glass windows, gothic structure, it was a "friggin" church—albeit a pimped-out one. I had no idea where I was going in the club, and I looked up and saw the DJ booth suspended in the middle of the air about the equivalent to a second floor. I walked up two flights of steps and into an area where the DJ booth was: a platform with the turntables suspended from strings.

I then saw Keoki, we shook hands, and I knew the night was about to begin. He told me it was about 10 minutes before I went on. With at least 2,000 to 3,000 people on the dance floor and 40 people in the DJ booth area, no one but my friends knew me. I was a kid from New Jersey. I wanted to prove myself to the NYC crowd. It was time to start my set. I played my first record, and after the third or fourth record, I had the top five DJ's in NYC coming up to talk to me. In that moment, I became DJ Evets (Steve backwards). I remember seeing my friends in the crowd, and the party was insane. It was pure ecstasy.

I ended up DJing at The Limelight for about a year with Keoki. His night was called Disco 2000. It was mostly run by Michael Alig, on whom the movie *Party Monster* was based. The actual amount of time I would get to DJ would be 20 minutes to an hour. It all depended on Keoki's mood and how the night was going. The fact that I was even able to do this as a former nobody was a dream come true.

Now, DJing was just the surface. So many things went on in this place that I cannot even mention, as it is so controversial and taboo. For a glimpse, I saw people masturbating in the open or doing cocaine on the DJ booth right in front of me. I was even caught a few times having sex in the bathroom. I was never into drugs. I told myself I would not snort anything or inject something with a needle. I have not to this day. The biggest drugs of the time were hallucinogens such as LSD and ecstasy. Like I said, I never snorted or injected anything, but with some of the things I did do, I am happy to be alive today.

I admit to experimenting with certain contraband. It really does affect the way I think today. That stuff messes with your memory and other things in your body. I could literally have a flashback on the spot just by thinking of what it felt like. Besides the drugs was the sex. I had a serious girlfriend back then, but we did stuff out in the open—in bathrooms, cars, and anyplace we could find. One time we were going at it in a stall, and I happened to look up to see a girl peeking over to watch us. I was so pissed off that I yelled at her. Meanwhile, we were doing it so often that security was placed in the bathroom at all times. Even when I was single, the amount of action I got from being in that scene was absurd.

I know I have always had a guardian angel, because some of the things I did back then could really have killed me, but this was all part of my experience and I learned from all the things I ever did. The people that used to go to these clubs were on talk shows because of how wild they were. People have died for many reasons related to that life, and these were the kids that ran the nightlife. A movie was made about this club and addressed how one of the Club Kids was murdered and how they found the man who did it. The guy who managed the club the night I was spinning was the murderer.

The contacts with the wild and controversial people I had in NYC were crazy. I spent a year of my life with The Limelight. I learned a very valuable lesson: *you could be yourself and still be accepted.* It opened my mind. My experiences at the clubs would continue to play a huge role in the choices I would make in the future and my decision-making process. The people in the clubs did not care what anyone thought about them. Their attitudes taught me a lot about self-confidence. These people did things that were taboo or acted to extremes and never cared when people mocked or made fun of them. They were who they were. Witnessing that as a young person, I learned to just be myself and pay no attention to what other people thought about me. I also realized that open-mindedness is important. Ultimately, nothing shocks me anymore. I learned to accept people's differences.

What Baby Boomers enjoyed as a mind-blowing experience at Woodstock is the same type of eye-opener the clubs gave me. Through the clubs and the people, I learned to be open and creative about my own ideas and artistic impressions (I am a very artistic person). I would use these early experiences and channel them into my future creative endeavors across multiple professions all throughout my life.

After about a year of DJing at the Limelight, the main DJ, Keoki, who had asked me to spin in the first place cut me off. He said that I was taking over his night and I did not fit his style. So he told me it was over. I was a little offended at first, but I realized I was lucky and grateful to have had the opportunity.

My stint as a DJ took its toll. I was fired from a day job. I was still in school so my grades suffered. I got home at 7:00 a.m. and had to go to school as soon as I walked in the door. I had made DJing my top priority. When I say I got fired, it is because I put my DJ career ahead of the other position. The manager at the other job asked me to make a choice: work there and quit my DJing or be fired. I chose the nightlife scene. I was making choices based on working in the clubs. It had become a sort of addiction. So when Keoki cut me off, it was an opportunity to walk away from what was essentially bringing me down.

I realized I was lucky to even be alive. In the time I worked in the club, I was in car accidents, put in dangerous scenarios with dangerous people, and so much more. I know I had a guardian angel protecting me, because man I probably should have died a long time ago.

DJing at The Limelight opened up a lot of local opportunities for me. After leaving The Limelight, I went on to DJ at local clubs in NJ. I continued DJing for at least another 15 years. It was very hard to balance school, work, and DJing. I loved the nightlife for the flashy things—popularity, women, music, confidence-boosters, and fame. But I started to realize it was taking over. I was beyond burnt out by the time it all finally ended, and I was ready to get out for good.

DJing is something that will always be a part of me. I learned so much about music from all different genres, and it was honestly something I loved. Even to this day, if I have an opportunity to DJ, I will do it just for the fun of it. But I cannot go back to the nightclub scene. It is a place that could suck me up with flashy colors and music, and take over my life again.

I would say the biggest thing I learned from DJing was being able to work a crowd, and by playing different types of music, I would get a variety of reactions. I would go to other clubs, observe other DJs, and learn how to play the crowd. Specifically, so they would always like me. That really helped me understand the power and control one could have based on decision-making skills. I learned that I had the ability to control emotions through my own decisions—and that is a huge part in business. Because whether I am giving a presentation, sharing a story, writing a book (hint, hint), I can control people's emotions and reactions. And that is one of the biggest takeaways I took from DJing. Making people cry, making them angry, and saving lives and maybe even my own.

I have always taken music seriously and learned how to control my own emotions through it. And as we get farther into the book, you will see how decision making and playing off people's emotions leads to growth.

There was a guy named Vinny with a badass Mohawk who used to come every week. I approached him and started talking to him and shared I was the main DJ. After learning what bands he liked, I started playing songs for him every week. He would come religiously just to hear me play ONE song for him. He then brought a bunch of people who all would wait just for that one song I would dedicate to them. So you see, connecting with people and understanding how your actions can trigger their emotions is priceless.

I was very fortunate to have loyal friends like George, Amon, and Jorge who were literally at almost every club and party I spun at during a certain time period. There are so many other people who were always there for me and showed support.

Are you tying this into business yet? In the earlier chapter, I started creating a name for myself. If you can remember from my school chapter, I talked about how I was learning the art of performing and communication. Being a DJ was the next phase in that personal growth. I was the main guy that people would come to see and escape the night through the music I played. Connecting with people, understanding people, adapting to the different groups that liked certain types of music—all of it was teaching me something to use later in my life.

I will never forget the nightlife days, and the DJ in me will always be there.

CHAPTER 4

JOBS

NOW THAT YOU ARE GETTING TO KNOW ME A BIT BETTER, I WOULD like to dive into my job history. Things in my life are going to get really interesting here. I have worked almost every type of job imaginable and took a lot of training courses in many fields.

Just to give you an idea of my lengthy job experiences, here is the list:

» Amusement park employee (first job)

» Nightclub DJ

» Food truck cashier

» Speaker sales out of a van

» Fire extinguisher service man

» Hair salon assistant

» Hairstylist

» Hair educator

» Security guard

» Multi-level marketer

» Firefighter

» Fugitive recovery agent

» Auxiliary police officer

» Videographer

» Promoter

» Customer service representative

» Entrepreneur

If I missed any jobs, these positions will surely come up during this chapter discussion. You probably are asking, "Why on Earth did he work so many different professions?" I understand the question. Trust me, it all contributed to my future success. Everything I have learned I then applied to my entrepreneurial activities. I believe that all of our past experiences shape our next job or career. It has been no different for me. So let's take a walk through some of my most memorable jobs and experiences.

In high school, my first job was working in an amusement park—a place located almost completely behind my house. This well-known park drew thousands of families. Most of my responsibilities included operating rides, cleaning up and walking around the property. Here I learned to take orders from people and accomplish specific tasks. I also learned a great deal about people, families, and children.

Its many children's rides attracted kids, of course. While I was shy back then and lacked communication skills, I was always polite and courteous to people. I was a teenager and prone to getting into trouble when the park slowed down. One time I crawled into one of the rides to take a nap only to be awakened by three managers. They stared and one said, "Is he seriously sleeping on the job?" Lesson learned: *never sleep on the job*; and besides, you should never doze off unless you are being paid to sleep.

This job lasted through high school and ended shortly after I graduated. That is when I started hanging around the wrong crowds and DJing at clubs in NYC. Part of the reason I changed directions so often was because I was not sure what I wanted to do with my life when it came to making a career choice or taking on a new job. For a long time, I relied on dollars earned from DJing at the clubs and parties—and that was not much money.

My mother always encouraged me to be continually employed. She said any money is better than $0. My mother instilled a real work ethic and edict that said: always work and earn. Her advice:

STOP COMPLAINING AND START EARNING.

I still have that work ethic. Where I think people fail is waiting for that next best job and earning no income in-between. You will not become successful doing it this way. Since I applied this belief to my life, I never stopped working, hence the reason I held so many different jobs.

Moving along, my next career move was to become a hairstylist. I never really wanted to become a stylist or even knew much about the industry. Then one day I spotted this hot woman hairstylist who worked at a salon down the street from where I lived. She drew me and enticed me to work in a salon. I used to cut my friends' hair for fun so I was actually somewhat familiar with how to cut hair, but did not have much interest in doing it as a career.

So I went into the salon looking to do anything for money like take out the trash or sweep up. Of course, my real intention was to get close to my crush—the hot woman who turned out to be 20 years older. She mistook me for a hairstylist. I told her and the salon owners I just graduated high school and was looking for a job. They offered me a position as a salon assistant, which I had no idea what that job involved, but I accepted the position anyway. I quickly learned a salon assistant is someone who washes hair, cleans up, and assists the stylists. Assistants are the backbone of any salon.

After working at this salon for a few months, they suggested that I get into the business and go to school to become a stylist. I was not doing much of anything else but living up the nightlife so I decided to enroll in the cosmetology program at the local Vo-Tech. If you can remember from my last chapter, I had to choose between a job and the nightlife. I bailed out on this job. My ego ruled that decision. I felt too cool to work at a salon when I was becoming a popular DJ and enjoying nightly partying.

As I shared in the last chapter, I eventually quit DJing and began to get serious about what I would do next. Giving up the DJ lifestyle and having the work ethic I just described, I realized I had to make some life choices. I decided to get back into the swing of things. I wanted to focus on my career over going out every night. I want to say something important: My girlfriend at the time who spent this part of the journey by my side was always supportive.

So now at age 20 it was time to get serious. I decided to become a full-fledged hairstylist. I remember attending my first hair show and being blown away by all of the action going on. This took place at a huge convention center with thousands of attendees from all over the industry. It really opened my eyes with regards to how big the salon world really was and could be.

I walked up to a booth and saw a guy in a suit on stage working on models. I thought, "*That* is what I want to do." He attracted a huge crowd around him—all beautiful women who gave him lots of attention. It was like being in show business. As I continued exploring my latest career option, I frequently saw this guy at a number of shows. I decided to approach him. I introduced myself to him and said that I wanted to do what he did for a living. Now, before we go any further there is a valuable lesson here:

DO NOT WAIT FOR THINGS TO HAPPEN. NO ONE IS GOING TO CHASE AFTER YOU.

I took the initiative to approach this guy. I felt very nervous when I went up to him. He said he had seen me before at other shows. He gave me his card. I left that show feeling a huge sense of accomplishment. Life lesson:

DO NOT LET FEAR RULE YOUR DECISIONS.
GO RIGHT TO THE SOURCE WHEN YOU WANT TO GET HELP.

A few days later, I called this man. He would later become my mentor and role model over the next five years. His name is Timothy Walker. I have not seen Timothy in a while. Every time I did see him, I always thanked him for everything he did to help me. He would always respond and say, "I did nothing; you did it all."

Getting back to doing what he did, I had to undergo a bunch of training and needed way more work experience in the field. Timothy was an educational director for a huge beauty company and worked with a local distributor. There were auditions taking place to be considered for employment at a place five months from that time. He went on to coach me and prepare me for that event. He put me in scenarios that I would question why. He pushed me to the limits like never before. He helped me understand and learn lessons in life and business.

I had to memorize a manual, which was about 80-pages long—and I had to do it word for word. Well, I did not have to do it, but it is what he suggested I do. Every night for the next five months, I would rehearse, study, and prepare myself for that big day. In the meantime, I still needed to find a job. This may blow your mind, but Timothy made me interview 75 salons and rate them from one to five—and I had two weeks to do it. I thought he was nuts at first, but I actually got it done. Some towns alone have about 20 salons in them so after a few days I was able to knock out 30 or so. I simply made an appointment with them and shared that I was looking for a place to work and was interviewing salons. I mostly went to salons in NJ and NYC. I went to all of the biggest salons in NYC to the smallest ones in NJ.

What I soon discovered became a lesson in and of itself. It was an eye-opening experience. From the operations, clients, money, and hours, it was all mind-blowing. One thing I do suggest is that when looking for a job, be sure to see what is out there. Take an adventure and interview other places and rate them in your own way. It really will open your eyes and mind.

I nailed down the top five then narrowed it down to *the* salon of choice. It was a local salon in Jersey that really did not have a whole lot going on, but for some reason I liked it the best. Tim also said it was the best one. For the first few months, I thought it could not get any better, but then things started to change. I was not happy with how I was being treated. The staff, atmosphere, all of it—I just did not fit in. I felt like an outcast for just being who I was as a person. I would go home at times feeling very upset and wanting to quit, but Tim said to stick it out.

At that time, my girlfriend was pregnant with my son, which I was keeping a secret from everyone since I was afraid they would judge me. I was 20 and was going to be a father, yet hardly had any money and was still so young. I would question in my mind why Tim would tell me to stay in a place I was miserable working in. Finally, after about a year, he said to jump ship and switch to a much better place than the last one. Of course, I trusted my mentor and started working at a new salon. This place was even smaller than the last, but it seemed great at the start. I almost skipped over the biggest job in my career as my five months of prepping was up. The day I had to make my presentation was here.

I had my suit on and was ready to present. I had no idea what to expect as I walked into a conference room that had three executives and three other people trying out for the job. Tim stood off to the side to observe. I ended up getting picked to go last. As I watched the others present I was close to having a panic attack. I had never given a presentation like this before. It was my turn.

I got up in front of the room and saw the other candidates as well as corporate staff. I introduced myself and started to recite the manual word for word as they followed along turning the pages while in shock. I can recall Tim having a huge smile on his face and being so proud of me. When I was done, they were pretty much speechless for a few minutes and said they have never heard anyone recite the entire manual to them. That statement was followed up with: "We see great things in your future, Stephen."

I got the job and my role was to travel to salons to teach the staff about hair-color theory and products. It was really a great experience. I learned the art of public speaking, customer relations, time management, and a whole slew of other skills. I went from having no job to having three jobs. I was still a DJ, but now I was also providing education and working in the salon as an assistant.

When I started at this new salon, it was in a different capacity. Tim personally recommended me to the owner, and they all had high regards for me right from the start. After a few months, this started to become all too familiar, as I once again became miserable. I just felt so different from the others, and this feeling perpetuated over the next few years. I went on to work for two more salons under Tim's direction until I could not take it anymore. I needed a break from him and wanted to run my own life. I lost touch from Tim as time went on, but he was there to see me become a father and was very supportive.

Tim taught me an important lesson. I questioned him later on why he put me in such bad jobs. His response (and I will cherish this for the rest of my life) is your takeaway:

"I SIMPLY WANTED YOU TO SEE THE BAD BEFORE YOU COULD APPRECIATE THE GOOD."

That lesson has literally saved my career time and time again. I hope you will learn and value it, too. I went from working in a number of other salons and companies, winning awards, and training thousands of people to where I am now. I can literally name and thank some of the people I worked for even though they may never read this book or even remember me: Susan, Toni, Bernadette, Lisa, Lucio, Nick and Sal, Jon and Debbie. I learned valuable lessons from all of them, including what *not* to do.

The salon industry was a great one for me. However, after about six to seven years in, I decided that I wanted to make a career change. I had lost my passion for this industry and wanted to pursue something I was always interested in as a young kid. I had always been fascinated with the military and anything regarding war in general. My childhood best friend, Rodney, and I used to buy toy guns and play war in the woods together. You would have thought we were in the jungles of Vietnam with how seriously we took this role-playing.

My goal was to go into the army, then college, then the FBI. I ultimately wanted to be in law enforcement, but I was not sure where to begin. Of course, my family advised against it since I had a young son. The idea did not seem to fit my lifestyle. I wanted to save lives and give back, so I learned that the local fire department was looking for new volunteers. I applied, got accepted, and went off to the fire academy.

At the time, I was still working part-time in a salon, but eventually got out 100 percent. I was only jobless for a month or two, but graduated from the academy and became an official firefighter. At this point, my life began to change. I went from being in a safe environment around 90 percent women to then being in life or death situations, saving lives and working with 90 percent men—that was big change for me.

I quickly wanted to continue on my career path into law enforcement, but really had no idea what to do. My brother, Pat, said that he saw a sign that a local police department was recruiting new officers. I immediately went in to find out more information. Before this particular job came into place, I had enrolled in a program to become a Deputy Sheriff's Officer, but then had to pay my own way and even purchase my own weapon. I purchased the weapon but then learned it would cost me over $3,000 to go through the academy, so I bailed out of that program. Another department paid for my way into the academy. I had picked up a job working as a part-time security guard just to get some experience.

The academy started in a few months, and I prepped myself for it as best I could. I remember the first day: I had to be there at 0600 hours. I felt very nervous and had no idea what to expect other than the rumors of being screamed at by the instructors. OC spray was the worst part of the academy. If you do not know what that is, it is basically a stronger version of mace specifically made for the police. What a nightmare—it was brutal how they introduced the spray. I made it through the academy and was enrolled in an Auxiliary Police role, which was a part-time program where I hoped to get hired.

Within a year's time of leaving the salon industry, I had already been through two academies and received numerous training certifications and even a few citations for service and rescue operations. I worked as a security guard and felt I was on my way to my goal.

The big picture was to join the FBI, but I had no idea how to apply for that type of job. So I decided to call the FBI. Yes, I looked up the number and literally called the FBI. I must have hit the jackpot because I got a local branch number and called. Someone answered, and I said that I would like to speak to someone who could provide me with information on becoming an agent. He said that I got the right guy on the phone—he was the Special Agent in Charge of that local unit. Remember what I said before?

ALWAYS GO RIGHT TO THE SOURCE AND DO NOT LET FEAR HOLD YOU BACK.

I asked him how I could become an agent. He shared all sorts of information with me that really opened up my mind. I had written an article for a website about two years ago entitled, "What I Learned About Marketing Applying to the FBI." So what did I learn? He suggested that I needed to look as good on paper as I could because they get thousands of applications on a regular basis and they all look the same after a while. This is why they started looking to hire accountants, computer science majors, lawyers, and people from other non-traditional backgrounds. They were flooded with criminal justice majors. Another valuable lesson:

ALWAYS LOOK GOOD ON PAPER!
I STAND BY THIS ONE.

Basically, you need to stand out from the rest and have a lot of experience in whatever it is you are looking to do or even experience in general. Now you can understand the value of holding and learning about so many different jobs. My diverse experience has made me who I am as a person and helped me to better manage just about any situation.

After my talk with him, I decided to send him a thank you letter. I called him back about a month later, and he actually thanked me for sending it in to him. Remember to look as good as you can on paper. Since this was many years ago, paper was the only thing you could look good on. Today there are so many digital platforms that you can shine on and many ways to showcase your work and experience. Back then, it was simply a résumé.

Later, I saw an ad looking for fugitive recovery agents, otherwise known as bounty hunters, in a local paper. I called up and faxed them my résumé. Thanks to the FBI Agent, I looked pretty good on paper. I went in for the interview in a suit and tie. I learned later that the other agents, most of whom were complete douche bags, made fun of me because presumably I took myself seriously, acted professional and wanted to be different from the rest. Isn't it crazy how you are sometimes looked down on for going above and beyond being average?

During my interview, they did mention how my resumé caught their attention with my diverse background and job history. I had a three-month probation period before I could carry a gun. Little did I know that this job was going to be a living hell.

I got the job and I was assigned to a power-hungry, egomaniac team of a-holes. My primary role, as well as the role of all the people in the office, was to hunt down people who missed their court dates and had warrants out for their arrests. In other words, they were fugitives on the run. They got arrested at some point, got bailed out, and went under the radar. It was our job to find them and bring them in. Sounds exciting, right? Well it was, but that is if you want that kind of lifestyle and work environment. We had a lead on a suspect, and it was my first time to go out in the field with my team. Before I go into the actual experience, let me share with you what this event entailed.

Someone gets arrested and then needs to get bailed out. Bail Bonds companies pay the bill, which is a loan, and it is up to the arrested person to pay it back and show up for their court dates. They skip out, and local authorities notified us. Our job involved going to find them and bringing them in. We most often only had a name and phone number of a relative or friend. They needed to list a co-signer or reference when they posted bail. We contacted that reference and had to persuade them to give up intelligence on the fugitive's potential location. On average, the references would not divulge that information. Sometimes though they ratted and gave up the information. I have seen all kinds of busts, from peaceful to aggressive raids in bedrooms with a wife and baby in the room standing by as we cuffed the fugitive.

The first job we went on I can recall being pretty amped up, but I did not know what to expect. Since I had official police training, I was used to some form of professionalism and organization. In this job, none of that experience applied. These types of guys in this field did not follow standard rules and procedures. As a new employee, my job required me to run the back of the house alone in the dark—most of our hits were around 3:00 a.m. to 4:00 a.m. I had to wait in case the suspect ran out of the back of the house at which point I would attempt to stop him.

I cannot tell you the number of fences I had to climb over, dogs that tried to attack me, and ridiculous situations I encountered. The front of the house presented risks, too. The overall job proved intense. I worked there only for a few months, but it was hell every day. I recall getting calls at 1:00 a.m. to go do a hit on a location in the middle of nowhere. They expected me to go wherever and whenever without complaint.

The worst situations involved guys who ran across country or traveled hours away, so I would have to sit and capture them. Afterwards, I would have to babysit the prisoner in some random hotel and then bring him to prison. Oh yeah, I forgot—we would have to bring the prisoners into the actual prisons; it was not a fun place to be. I saw some crazy-ass people in there and would never want to be in that environment.

Before we move on to what I learned from this particular job, allow me to share the moment I realized that I needed to get out; it was one the scariest moments of my life. We had a lead on a suspect (I believe in the Bronx), and we decided to pay a visit to where he was suspected to live. It was in a bunch of apartments, and his unit was located somewhere in the middle of the development on the first floor. They assigned me, as usual, to the back. I approached a 10-foot-tall fence and radioed in to ask which apartment the suspect was in. I wanted to get a visual and the fence was an obstruction. They ordered me to climb over the fence and get into position.

I had a bad feeling about the situation, as the walkway was about four feet wide and ran in-between all the apartments' back-yards on the left and right. I climbed over the fence and began to advance toward the apartment about 12 units ahead on the left from where I stood. Many of the fences were protected by wood and some were plain fences. As I began to slowly walk up, a dog viciously came at me from the right, and I had forgotten there was a fence there. The dog was trying to gnaw through the fence and attack me. Then, one from the left side started barking and jumping at me, then again on the right. Before I knew it, about 12 dogs on the right and left side of me surrounded me—all of the animals were barking and aggressively trying to attack me. I was literally shitting a brick and pulled out my OC spray to keep them back. I had gotten to the spot I needed to be in and I radioed that I was in position. They advised to fall back to the car; the suspect was not there. I had to walk back, climb over the fence, and make it back to the car. I managed to and shared my story with them, but of course, they could have cared less. It was "part of the job." As I sat in the car I knew that I did not want to or need to be around assholes like these guys, nor did I want that job anymore.

What did I learn from that job? I learned the art of getting information out of people, how to track people down with very little information and learn when people are lying, hiding something or making stories up. I learned how the court system works. I learned how to work with informants to get intelligence, and most importantly, how to treat people. If you act professionally and treat someone humanely, it can prevent many situations from happening. One time a suspect actually thanked me for being nice and showing him respect. See, even when dealing with criminals, you can still provide a great experience and good customer service. Treating people the way I do has saved me on a number of occasions where I could have taken an aggressive approach, and it would have not been a pretty ending.

Since we are on the topic of public safety, I did put about six years combined working in fire and law enforcement. I worked at a reserve unit where I performed typical police and firefighting work. I have saved a few lives and most of the time it was simply calming people down and making them feel comfortable. It seems in all aspects of life that skill can make everyone feel better. If you know me personally, it is something that I rarely talk about, and most people are shocked to hear that I worked in the public safety field.

I did not continue this line of work. It had started to change me. I did not like who I was becoming. Although I gave back and did acts of service, the job itself and the people it attracted did not mix well with my personality and values. I found myself in many scenarios where the way some of these people handled matters just did not work for me. I realized the public safety profession attracted a certain type of person, and I was not cut out for the culture of these types of jobs. I did however learn some of the most valuable characteristics and skill sets from working in that environment such as, the ability to be razor focused, do anything I can to get the job done, and be extremely strategic in accomplishing any goal. The training alone that I went through was very intense. I was trained in confined space operations, rescue operations, 911 dispatcher training, weapons training, and a variety of other skills needed for the job.

Shortly after 9/11 happened, I had a wakeup call. When the towers were hit, I was actually called in to patrol for white vans and terrorists. Talk about being freaked out! No one had any idea what could happen next. Our home soil was attacked! I will never forget the resulting smell of the bodies, the burning, the smoke, and aftermath of 9/11 just from driving on the Pulaski Skyway. I even went to get my son out of school just to have him safe with me.

I made a decision and wanted to go back into the salon industry. I did not want to put my life on the line anymore and wanted to be in a profession I once was good at as well as using a craft I worked hard to learn about many years ago. The first place I called was a salon that was looking for a stylist not too far from where I lived. I went in and shared how I was out of the industry for some time and how I used to be skilled, but was just rusty.

The owner, Jon, decided to hire me and I spent about eight years with him. He was a great guy and ran a very tight ship. I learned a lot from him and was fortunate to have built up a nicely sized clientele. As was the case with most jobs I had, I started to lose motivation and became unhappy. I decided to leave and moved to a salon about 15 minutes away. I left on somewhat bad terms, but since then we have forgotten the past and became friends again.

I moved to a salon that is owned by Debbie, whom I promised I would mention in this book. Debbie was super supportive when it comes to managing my own business and seeing my clients at this location a few days a week. There are times I question if I should still work in a salon because I am just getting too busy, but I love my clients and making people feel great about how they look. Many of my clients have been a huge influence on my brand and have been so good to me over the years. With technology the way it is today and social media, you can connect with people like never before and keep them all up to date on what you are doing.

On the subject of technology, I started the first ever search directory for salons on the Internet back in 1999 with an old friend. I later went on to create my own site called salonsearch.com, which was a database of salons where people could view the salon and any information they needed before booking an appointment. I wanted to create a way to help people find quality salons. I will get into technology later in the book, but this was the first actual business I owned. I created an LLC in 1999 and called it Stephen Gabriel Designs. I named it after my son. SalonSearch still exists; however, it is not my main focus now. I will dive deeper into this in my business chapter.

At the start of this chapter, I mentioned some of the jobs I had—and they were all a learning experience. I learned a lot about sales, especially trying to sell food out of a truck and speakers out of a van. These jobs did not last long at all, in fact maybe less than a week, but I learned how aggressive people can be when selling. It was such a valuable lesson because I saw how often they would get turned down and how people would be very harsh toward salespeople. From those short-term jobs to career changes, I pretty much have been in any and every situation you can be in. From wearing uniforms to suits, I do not regret any of my jobs.

Moving to the year 2000, I went through a major tragedy, which I will get into later. This inspired me to start a new journey in my career. I still hold this job today and it is my ultimate passion and business. I created *TheSalonGuy*. At first, I had a blog, but I was not even sure what blogging was about. I would watch videos on YouTube about people I looked up to and would always search for motivational videos. I came across a video on how to turn what you love into a business. This stage in the game played out to be a huge part of my growth and brand.

I was inspired by reading a book on the topic of turning your passion into a business—and I was hooked. New doors opened for me and this was a way for me to expand on what I loved: people. I have always been a people person, loved technology, and had a huge interest in business. I launched this endeavor just as the web was becoming a huge resource for companies and brands to make platforms for pretty much anything. I decided to follow the steps in the book, and to this day, I owe it all to that book. For the last six years,

I have been busting my ass to create a brand and business for myself, and this has been my favorite job so far.

There are so many people that are lost when it comes to finding out what they want to do. Have you ever felt stuck in a rut and simply hated going to a job where you have no passion? It is more common than you think; just no one admits it. It is not easy figuring out how to find out what you love, let alone the job you have been dreaming about since you were 15, but later in the book I will share the best formula that will help you find your true passion and how you can work in that environment. The key is NOT waiting around for something to happen. You seriously need to hustle and bust your ass like never before. It is a whole new adventure and something that can only be done by having lots of passion and dedication.

Your job should reflect who you are as a person and what you believe in. Why not work for a company that you love rather than just taking a job to have one. Yes, I know it is a paycheck, and yes, that is super important; but in my life, I always went for emotional happiness over just having a job. This is why I jumped from career to career and job to job. I was trying to find what I could connect with, and I finally did as I got older and smarter. I went through a shit load of horrible situations, emotions and feeling lost, but they all contributed to my knowledge and what you are reading has all come from these experiences.

One thing that always is important when it comes to jobs is money. Money has been my best friend and worst enemy. I used to make good money when I was younger between DJing in clubs, working in a salon and teaching part time. There are times I feel I made more money back then compared to now! Money can be the root of all emotions. I had so many struggles with money and it is always something I never really talked about or shared with people. It is very common these days to hear people share how much they are making, but I do not talk about it. I once told myself I was the richest poor guy. I went through so many financial struggles while at the same time making a lot of money. We are not talking BIG money; I just always had something coming in. I worked very hard for my money, and as you know, all jobs pay differently. I understand how people could survive off $400 a week about 20 years ago, but now if you do not make that in a day, you are going to have a tough time living. I also happen to live in New Jersey, which is ridiculously expensive. Even to live in NYC, you need have a great paying job just to afford to live there. Money controls everything, and there are so many people out there having a hard time living paycheck to paycheck. The challenge is that many people complain about their lives and jobs and do not know what to do about it. This is where what I am sharing with you will inspire you to make a change for yourself and your career.

This chapter has been very important. I have now shared what I have been through professionally to show that success is not landing one job at the age of 21 and working at the same job for 30 years—or is it? If you want to be an entrepreneur, then you need to actually be one and make the sacrifices and changes needed to get ahead. Get out of that crappy miserable job and make a change in your life. I know it does not sound easy, and it is not, but you can and will have the knowledge to do it after you read this book.

CHAPTER 5

RELATIONSHIPS

FROM FAMILY FEUDS TO ONE-NIGHT STANDS, RELATIONSHIPS have been a rollercoaster of emotions and experiences in my life. Since I was a baby, I was in an unhealthy environment and was lucky enough to be taken out of it early enough to be saved from an unstable upbringing. Despite the bad shit that happened, I always have been fortunate enough to build relationships with people who have been a huge inspiration to my life and career.

Family, work, and partners are all different, but they are all part of the relationship cycle we all go through. Typically, when a relationship ends, we tend to feel sad, alone, and unsure of the reasons why it ended. I have blamed myself many times for the end of a relationship and I think it stems back to my childhood where my biological mother pretty much neglected me and kept me guessing about her. Relationships can be the root of many emotions whether good or bad. Have you ever been in a relationship and felt so miserable that you felt trapped? This has happened to me in a job and with girlfriends.

Let's start with family. I was very lucky to be adopted by the Marinaro family, attend private school all my life and be taken care of and supported by my family. I mentioned earlier that I have a small disconnect from them since we do not share DNA and act differently, which is quite common with adopted families. Despite these differences, my family has been there for me in all ways.

In the last chapter, I mentioned how money is the root of evil—and in my family, this issue existed. Those who have the money have the power. My family helped me out financially on several occasions, but I still feel horrible about it. I cannot think of a worse feeling than owing someone money. It is a heavy burden that weighs me down. I feel you cannot get rid of it unless you become super rich. It is a shame but money can even control families. I did not necessarily come from money, but I was raised in a very stable environment, and everyone always worked. I learned early on about working multiple jobs to make ends meet.

My family showed me and exposed me to pretty much all aspects of life and work. My sisters in particular really set me up well in terms of learning about music, movies, and the arts. For example, when my sister, Mary Lu, had a rock band in the early 80s, I used to go to gigs and help her carry the equipment then watch her sing and play piano. I learned at an early age about sound equipment, music, and how she dealt with people. My sister, Carmelyn, always played classic rock in her car. I hated it at first, but now am so happy I heard those songs over and over. Today those songs have become the basis of much contemporary music you hear.

She was also a huge movie buff and used to work at local cinemas where my best friend or I would even go solo to watch movies like it was nothing. The coolest part was that we were treated like 10-year-old VIPs. If you knew Carm, the staff treated you differently. You got anything you wanted, and we pretty much lived in the theaters.

My brother, Pat, left the house early so I did not see him as much, but I felt cool to be around him. At one point, he worked as an architect and taught me about buildings and projects. He managed big building projects and sometimes took me to see some of them. He is my "big bro" even though I rarely see him due to distance. I also had a great relationship with my brother-in-law Frank, Mary Lu's husband. He treated me as his own and looked out for me. I learned a lot about cars, outdoors stuff, and how to not put up with shit. Actually, I got that from my *whole* family!

As I grew up, I started to see the differences in my personality and traits compared to my family. It is just about differences, not what is good or bad. As I matured, I started to come into my own sense of self. I tend to be a loner and keep my distance from others. I hate that part of myself sometimes, but it also allows me to get things done. I work like a beast, and I can do it best on my own. I would see and still see all of my cousins at family events. Everyone accepted me from a young child as part of the family, and I am forever thankful for that. I had no other family but this one. From all the trips and fun adventures to the family dinners we would all be at. I even had a great relationship with my best friend Rodney's family as a child, and his family also treated me like one of their own. I am thankful and blessed to have these experiences. People liked me because I was a good kid, a jokester, and I showed everyone respect.

Relationships stem from all aspects of life experience, such as business, lovers, best friends, family, co-workers, and even pets. I learned a lot from relationships and the aftermath of ones that did not work out so well.

Let's go back to school for a minute. I loved girls since birth and probably even winked at a nurse when I was just born! As you will recall from the earlier chapter, I was quite the "ladies' man" in grade school. Remember that "proposal" in second grade? Well, that has an interesting side story to it. Since I went to Catholic school, I figured the church was right there and it would have been an easy process. To make things even better, I snuck in my mother's jewelry box and took a ring I saw to give to my new "wife."

During our ceremony in front of the school and about eight other classmates, I put the ring on her finger, and we made it official. I do however think she filed for divorce by 3:00 p.m. I got home to my mother asking me if I gave a girl at school a ring. I eventually admitted it and learned that the ring I took was her actual engagement ring that my father had given to her when he proposed. Heck, how was I supposed to know! Of course, I had to ask her to return it—oops! So after we got *divorced*, we remained friends and ended up graduating together and moving on in life.

All throughout school, my focus was more on girls than actual school. What can I say? I had blonde hair, blue eyes, and a charming swagger. This lasted for about 10 years, and unfortunately is long gone just like my hair. Women have played such a *huge* part of my life. I feel like I have spent so much time, energy, and emotions on women I could actually retire from them. Trust me when I say I *love* women, but at this stage my preferences have changed so much that I am more focused on my business stuff and living a healthy lifestyle that it has now become the least most important thing in my life.

My love life has been full of ups and downs. I even unfortunately have somewhat of a reputation of being a flirt and "womanizer," but that does not faze me because I know who I am and what I do better than anyone. Part of building relationships in any aspect of life requires some sort of charm and finesse. People judge each other mostly on behavior, attitude, and personalities so if you are lacking in any of those areas, most likely you will face some challenges in life.

Sometimes it takes flirting, being charming, and going the extra mile, but the key is to be *real* and be you. People can spot a fake very easily. Now back to girls. I admit to having been with a LOT of women. Some relationships lasted years, months, days and even hours sadly. Ninety percent of most intimate relationships I have had with women originated in the club scene. Some were long term, and some short, but my element was the club and bar setting (plus girls always wanted to hang with the DJ).

I want to share love with someone. As I have matured, there are so many more important values that I look for in a person. It is not about how attractive they are; it is more about building trust and having a great relationship with that person that covers all aspects. My heart has been broken plenty of times, and it was always painful. Probably one of the worst feelings we can experience is heartbreak. You have to create an emotional border to where you protect yourself from any heartbreak. This applies to *any* relationship. You can be let down in business as well as personally.

HERE IS A LESSON ABOUT RELATIONSHIPS: THEY COME AND GO.

I have met thousands of people in my life; many of whom I never speak to anymore, never see, only met once or twice, or even only had a casual introduction with. Our life revolves around relationships. You need to prepare yourself to expect them to not last long. Family is most important as they will always be a part of your life, but it is very common to lose that bond and connection as time goes on. From children not talking to their parents to siblings hating each other, it is a part of life and happens on a regular basis. Prepare yourself for this so you are not as easily let down or upset.

As a single guy, I find myself missing companionship, romance, and passion. On the other hand, I have all the freedom in the world, which is a great feeling. Relationships can be financially and emotionally draining. Trust me, I have spent ridiculous amounts of money on women. Much of it was spent out of love and much on wining and dining. Nowadays if I want to go on a date, I would rather meet at Starbucks or a café and talk for an hour or so to get to know the person, which only would cost say about $10 compared to a $150 dinner when you feel it was a waste afterwards.

As I mentioned before, women have been a huge part of my life. Many have come and gone. I am actually okay with being single now as divorce rates are higher than ever, and it is more acceptable now to be single as you get older. It is a risky investment in my opinion. Do it only if you are SURE you are ready and found the right one.

As an entrepreneur, it is very difficult to focus on a relationship UNLESS:

» You have so much money you can live it up anytime and any way you want.

» Your partner is supportive and understanding of what you do and who you are.

» Your partner inspires you and motivates you to keep pushing forward.

» Your partner has similar goals and is hard working like you.

You must do a relationship audit. Look at the people you surround yourself with. If they are full of drama, live their lives on the edge, unstable, and always negative, trust me, you will become that as well. Get out of those relationships, environments, and lifestyles.

**IT IS LIKE THEY SAY, "YOU ARE WHAT YOU EAT."
I SAY, YOU ARE WHOM YOU HANG AROUND.**

This is why I have become much more of a loner these days. I have a small group of close friends, like 2–3 people, and I hardly go out to events or hang out anymore. I simply am too busy growing the relationship with myself. I have learned you can only rely on yourself as you will have many upsets and let downs. In business, you will have to rely on others in the beginning, but then you need to learn how to do EVERYTHING on your own. I learned how to shoot video, edit, take photos, do web design, and many more skills. Read books and learn as much as you can so that you can only let yourself down. Relying on others can be just as much of a disappointment as you can imagine. Only you can work as hard as yourself, and most people do not work that hard. I will talk about this later on in my chapter on business.

My best advice on relationships is to go through what you need to, but then focus on being happy with yourself. Become your best friend, learn how to explore your own fantasies, learn how to do what makes you happy, and never let anyone take that away from you. Learn a new craft, travel, wine and dine, do things that build your relationship with yourself.

I have achieved what I have thus far by not only building relationships with key people, but also with God. No matter what religion you are, we all end up praying to one hierarchy—and that is God. No one knows who God is, what God is, or where God is, but we all have one common connection and that is there is a source that controls everything. I myself went to Catholic school from Pre-K all the way through high school. Religion was taught to us as a class and was very strict.

I only really learned about my connection with God and embracing my beliefs when I was in my mid-20s. It was so random. It happened by meeting someone who explained it to me in a totally different way than I had learned in school. I almost felt guilty to think of a different way to connect with God, but this actually made more sense and I felt better.

It was a simple approach of just knowing God loves you, is always there for you, and wants the best for you. I mean it is so basic and general as well as so simple to embrace. At this stage in my life, I owe almost everything that has happened to me in the last 20-plus years to my connection with God and my beliefs. I literally have had miracles happen to me—things that can only be explained by having faith and putting out good energy into the world. Situations when I was on the verge of giving up and going into panic mode to when a miracle would intervene, not by luck, but by faith. I *strongly* suggest connecting with a higher power and creating a routine every day to where you connect with God or whomever you believe in. It will change your life, attitude and good things will start to happen.

Here is my ritual on a daily basis:

» Wake up, say a prayer, bless myself with Holy Water and a few memorable items; pray that I have a safe day; and pray that my family and friends are protected as well.

» I pray EVERY time I get into my car to keep me safe and protected; I do this every time I travel and with anything that involves me going somewhere.

» I pray every night before I go to bed. I have a prayer that I recite in my mind that includes keeping me safe and protected while I sleep as well for my friends and family.

» I thank God for everything I have and what happened that day.

» I also pray for when something big is going to happen such as a huge video shoot, project, meeting, or any opportunity that comes my way.

I do these things every day/night.

The best and biggest advice I can give when it comes to the topic of belief (if this is the only part of this book you take away) is this:

DO NOT QUESTION WHY, DO NOT BLAME GOD, AND DO NOT QUESTION WHY ANYTHING HAPPENS IN YOUR LIFE—GOOD OR BAD.

WE cannot control what happens nor do we have any ideas as to what will happen to us. Only God knows what our path is; therefore, we must be *thankful* for everything that happens. This is going to be hard at first and will be very difficult if you live your life filled with drama and negativity day by day, but over time, things will start to change. You literally have to let down your guard and become vulnerable to letting anything enter into your life. At this point, I only think of positive things; therefore, mostly positive things come into my life. You cannot control when, how or where, but just be open. This has been the biggest key of my success and growth thus far. Promise me you will do this and build a relationship with your higher power you believe in and be thankful for anything that comes your way—good or bad.

GOD IS YOUR BIGGEST INVESTOR.

CHAPTER 6

BUSINESS

THIS IS ONE OF THE CHAPTERS THAT I REALLY LOOKED FORWARD to writing. This chapter will really inspire and help you connect the dots as to where all of my storytelling has led. If you are an entrepreneur or someone toying with the idea of starting a business, launching a new brand or establishing something different in your life, this chapter will certainly help you.

In the previous chapters, I shared the variety of jobs I held which really opened my mind. I observed the many ways of doing business and what stood out most was the people part of it—the relationship building, customer service, hustling, and story about the brand. I call this: *How to do business while being human. Everything* you do revolves around how you treat and engage with people. I always gravitated toward older or successful people and sought them out myself. Till this day, I ask questions. The best thing you can do when you are in the company of someone successful is to ask questions. I have learned so much by doing this.

When I started my first business back in 1999, it came from an idea, a concept. Then I learned everything through executing it. Fear was not an option even though it was something no one else had done. Unfortunately, the *relationship* part of it caused me to break away and go on my own. That does not mean the person was bad or I played the blame game, but life will tell you what to do if you have faith and listen. Going on my own was a good choice for *me.* Did it work out better? Still not sure, but I do believe it happened for a reason and that it was meant to be.

There are so many aspects of doing business these days. You could be a business person by being a social-media star, starting or owning a line of whatever it is you want to sell, creating an online magazine or literally doing anything you want these days. It seems almost anything can be turned into a business. The difference between entrepreneurs is based on why he/she started it, the struggles he/she went through and his/her success story. These are the biggest differences from a real entrepreneur versus someone only looking for overnight success. It is easier to be famous for a year or two than to build up something from nothing over many years.

As I have grown professionally, there have been so many people I met that have little to no substance and are all about the fame and publicity. It is not obvious to everyone, but I can see it a mile away. All these people that are famous today will probably not be a few years from now. It really pains me to say that, and I only wish success for people, but it really comes from within. Let's look at a huge part of my current platform that contributes to my success: YouTube.

There are a crap load of "YouTubers" popping up on a daily basis. You can literally create an account, pick a hobby, get a camera, and start making videos. It's easy to start when you live at home, hardly have any bills, and have it easy. Many of these bedroom/bathroom bloggers are making big noise in the business world. Again, I hate to say this, but when you strip the layers away from what they do, what are you left with? You need to have an actual story of why you started what you started. Many people do not look at what they do as an actual business—and that is the BIGGEST difference.

Most of these people focus just on numbers not business. They get wrapped up in networks and people trying to land them deals or being controlled by other people. Do not get me wrong, it is awesome if you can do it and have a good run, but if you strip away all you have done, or what people are doing for you and you see what you are left with, much of it will be short lived and have little to no substance. I am about to be the harshest I will be in this book, but here it goes. When it comes to business, I am very passionate. Some situations I find disagreeable—and what I am about to share I do not like.

It is very easy to live at home, pay no rent, and start a YouTube channel. It is when you become an actual adult, have kids, buy a house, go to college, etc.—that is when shit gets real. Could you afford to pay $3,000 to $5,000 a month in bills? There are loads of multi-millionaires that got there from YouTube and that is beyond amazing, but look at how many musicians had one-hit wonders and are now broke and barely remembered. The point of all this is: no matter where you are in your life, have the following things in check.

» Why are you doing what you are doing?

» How do you do it?

» How can you make money from it?

WHY?

Let's start with the "Why" first.

In 2010, I had reached a point where I had become stagnant and lost a bit of passion for what I was doing as a hairstylist. Heck, as I mentioned previously, I even changed careers! Something was missing from my life and career and I had to make a change. I realized that working for other companies was not going to get me there. I needed to find a way to do something that others could not do for me.

My main goal was to create something that revolved around me where I could educate and inspire people. During that time, Mother became very ill and later passed away. It was a traumatic experience. Instead of going into a dark, depressing hole, I chose to use the strength, courage, and motivation that she instilled in me to accomplish a goal; I was not going to let anyone stop me or get in my way. I had already begun working on "TheSalonGuy" about a year or so before she passed; however, I had no idea what it was going to become.

I created a blog, which was the new thing to do for online exposure and content at the time. I even had other experts contribute to it. I had gained a bunch of attention from other people in the industry who provided tips and also gave me heads up on people not to trust and to steer clear of. The politics and backstabbing that went on were mind blowing. With not knowing who was who, I took a chance and dove into the realm of Internet marketing and blogging to gain exposure. I did not put a whole lot of effort into it, as I was very unsure of what I really had or what I needed to do.

So when my mother passed away, that was when I knew it was time to make a change and that I had something that I was not going to give up on. THIS is the real turning point for me.

I always did research online and was a big YouTube guy. I researched anything from tech stuff to motivational videos and that was a huge resource. I searched for motivational videos and came across a video from a guy named Gary Vaynerchuk. It was from a Web 2.0 conference where he did a keynote speech. The context of the video focused on why you should "stop doing shit you hate." Now, it was not that I hated what I did, but I sure was getting bored and tired of the same old environment within my industry. His speech not only hit home, but it was one of the biggest driving factors in starting my journey with my brand; the brand that I really had not even started or knew what to do with. I learned about his book *Crush It* and that was what really pushed me to get started and to turn my passion into a business. This book has helped thousands, if not millions of people. I am fortunate enough to be featured in his newest book *Crushing It!* His speech from that video impacted me so much that I started sharing it with other people. He just had this in-your-face-no-bullshit approach that really hit home and woke me up. So I read his book and followed his advice pretty much step by step.

One thing about me that really is hard for even me to grasp is that I have this crazy ability to be so dedicated and committed to something; it is like I literally turn on a switch. My own self almost possesses me and nothing gets in my way or steers me away from what I have my mind set on. This works with dieting also. For example, one day I will wake up, read or see something that just causes me to turn off that switch, and leave it off. I might read something about carbs, breads, snacks, drinking or something that would cause weight gain and I literally will eliminate all of those things from my life without hesitation, difficulty, or resistance and be dedicated to doing it for weeks. I WISH I could do it on demand or really understand how I do it, but it has helped me tremendously. The only challenge is that weeks will go by and then that commitment will wear off and then it is back to doing what I cut out. I then try to engage my mind but I just cannot do it. Tying this back into business, I decided to turn ON that switch and be more than dedicated to following Gary's advice. Before I get into the HOW, there are a bunch of things that I need to point out.

Being an entrepreneur is VERY difficult. You have to make sacrifices that the average person does not want to make. Sure, you can read books, be inspired, watch videos, etc., but 90 percent of people do not want to go the extra mile, make the lifestyle changes, hustle, or be patient when it comes to creating a business or brand. Trust me when I say I have made so many changes in my life to get to where I am that it depresses me at times. You are probably asking yourself how could success create depression. How can you be lonely? How many sacrifices do you REALLY have to make? Did you ever wonder why so many successful, talented actors, musicians, or athletes become depressed and end up having emotional challenges in their lives? It is because success can sometimes do that.

The key to not allowing that problem to happen is to live a life that creates a positive energy source and a rewarding one. You cannot welcome substances into your life that will cause you to go into a dark, deep hole. It was not uncommon for me to have a drink every night, from a few glasses of wine to a glass of scotch. However, I could physically and mentally feel how it affected me that night and the next day. I would wake up tired, sluggish, and I would just want to sleep more. I got fed up of feeling that way so I decided to just STOP drinking. As I am writing this, I have not had a drink in over four weeks. Till date, it's been over 2 years. I have had the occasional glass of wine or two, but that is rare. I just stopped cold turkey because I put my mind to it. This is not easy for everyone, but that is the power of the mind and what you need to do when it comes to building your business.

You need to make the effort and sacrifices that will create a better lifestyle for you. When I say lifestyle, I mean in general, as this will be the most exhausting thing you have ever done. Be prepared to work at least 14 hours a day, get only four hours of sleep a night, and put in the most effort you ever have in your life. Remember, this is all about YOU and your dreams. I had no idea what I was getting myself into nor did I have a real dream, but after reading Gary's book, I knew I had to do something.

There is a lot to share when it comes to building a brand and a business, and I am going to provide as much of what I have learned over the years as possible. Let's get back to the "why" part of this chapter. Why do you want to do something different in your life? Why do you need to make all these changes in your life? Why do you have to make sacrifices? Wait a second. Why can't I go to happy hour every night with my friends? Can I still go out to clubs four nights a week? Can I still watch four hours of reality TV every night? Well sure you can! If you want to be in the same place you are in five years from now. This is what makes this so difficult.

The average person does not need or want to give those things up. We all have total control of our lives and where we put our efforts. If you want to spend one hour a week on building up something for yourself, then you may be in it for the super long haul. If you want to spend 10+ hours a week, or 40+ hours, then that is a different story. The best single piece of advice I can give is:

YOU GET WHAT YOU PUT IN.

If you are lazy and sit around doing nothing all day, well guess what? That behavior will become your life. If all you do is go on social media and post nothing but drama, pictures of your cleavage, or pictures of yourself out partying, well guess what kind of attention and energy you will bring to yourself. You really need to look at what image you portray. You need to put your efforts and beliefs out into the universe before you can commit to anything. It will not be easy, but I can assure you it will be well worth it.

Be prepared to detach from close friends, mutual friends, family and pretty much become somewhat of a loner. This also really depends on how deep you want to go with this. There is absolutely nothing wrong with working a nine-to-five job and living a normal and fun social lifestyle. Trust me, I was a party animal and super social, but I went from that to pretty much becoming a loner.

If putting in two hours a week into something you love doing as a hobby is all you want to do, then AWESOME. You have to DO IT, though. Talking about it will not get you far. Focus back on WHY. Why do you want to make a change in your life? Do you need more money? Are you bored with your current job or career? Do you just want to try something different at this stage in your life? Whatever it is that you want to do, understand *the why* behind it. Then, decide how badly you want it. Most people give up at a certain point and just go back to their old lifestyle. Again, this path is not for everyone and that is fine, but if you really want it, you can make it happen.

Want to know why I decided to take on this journey of building a brand and business? One of the biggest reasons was because someone told me I would not be popular unless I was already a big name. I was basically told I could not do it right from the start. At first, I was floored and even hurt, but then I turned that hurt into drive and fuel. Most of the time people will tell you that you cannot do something. It will come from close friends, family, and even strangers. This is a very interesting topic to me as I have had many encounters with this topic titled: *Someone telling you that you cannot do something.*

Has that ever happened to you? It can be very hard to hear, but so many of today's biggest success stories come from being told they could not do it. I have learned that doing what you love and having passion for it is important, but you need to be REALISTIC with yourself and your mission. This mindset is crucial. You could spend years trying to achieve something that is just not cut out for you. For example, you could LOVE golf, love getting out to play, and even be good. However, chances are you might not be playing for the tour. You could spend years of playing and dreaming, but unless you are willing to put all the sacrifices in and really be committed, it could be a long, drawn-out hobby that could cost you time and money.

Life is very competitive, especially in sports. In business, however, we all have the ability to create something based around our hobbies and interests. I decided to take the leap simply because I was told no. I already knew that I had a passion for the industry I was in; however, I NEEDED to do something different. A huge factor was that I took the time to research being motivated and followed the proper steps to becoming successful. I also discovered a handful of people that became role models and even mentors. I read books, watched videos and movies, attended events, and did everything I could to really be inspired and educated.

My *why* was because I HAD to do something. I had lost the woman who raised and adopted me and then discovered a random guy on YouTube giving a speech on how to follow your passion, which was a wake-up call. Your whys can also change and become altered over time. You may decide to take on something because you want to try a new hobby, but it may later develop into something that is based off motivating, educating, or inspiring people. Much of what you choose to do should have an effect on people in a positive way. Thinking of others and how you can help them is a great way to fuel your passion and new journey. Think of the cause in what you want to do and how it can affect people.

Everyone lives under an emotional roof these days. Touching someone's emotions has become and has always essentially been a big part of business. Steve Jobs talked about how having the ability to touch someone's heart was the most important factor when he was creating the iPod. I totally agree on this because actions are fueled by emotions. There are tons of "Internet gurus" that boast their titles as Marketing Specialists, CEOs, Social Media Experts, blah blah blah, but in reality all they are trying to do is get you to their landing page that scrolls down for five years trying to sell you their eBook on how to be successful. Have you ever followed someone on Twitter because of his or her "expert" title, but then got an auto responder two minutes after being linked to a sales landing page? I absolutely HATE auto responders. Later in this chapter, I will list out a number of key essentials that I feel are dos and don'ts when it comes to business.

FEAR FACTOR

A lot of building a brand or business comes down to having one main characteristic—courage. Has fear ever held you back from something? What if I told you that I could eliminate the word "fear" from your vocabulary and you would never have to be held back by it ever again? Good news; I am about to do so.

So fear is probably the number one thing that holds us all back. It used to hold me back until a few years ago when something clicked within me. I asked myself what fear really is. It is just a challenge that you can and WILL overcome. There is a difference between being afraid when watching a horror movie and being scared of starting something that is your own thing, such as a business, or overcoming a challenge.

REPEAT THIS IN YOUR HEAD: A CHALLENGE THAT YOU CAN OVERCOME.

From now on, you will look at fear as a challenge that you can and will overcome. And here is the best part that will change your life. Fear should be afraid of YOU. Yes, fear is scared that you will overcome it and win the challenge. Fear is so scared that you will win. In most cases, if you have the drive to take it on and win, *it*, not you, will lose in the end. If you follow this mindset from now on, you will be amazed on how you can break free from what holds you back. In fact, I want you to erase the word fear from your mind. Everything from now on is a **challenge**—one that you can and WILL overcome. Nothing can hold you back now other than yourself. Fear is not an option. Failure is not an option. Promise me that you will practice this from now on in your life.

How does this all tie into business and building a brand? Well once you eliminate the one thing that holds you back from pushing forward, the sky is the limit. You can be free of fear and failure and that is the time to put your plan of action together. Remember to use your spiritual source, your guardian angel, your emotions, your pain, or your lowest of lows. Everything that has brought you down will be your fuel to push forward.

THE LOWS AND HIGHS

Let's talk about lows for a bit. I once heard from Tyson Beckford, "Your lows will determine the height of your success." I almost fell over when I heard that phrase. I have literally said that to not only myself, but to anyone else who has the challenges of lows. What does that mean, though? How low is low? Trust me when I say far down to the bottom of your emotional pit. There WILL be a point in your life where you feel nothing could get any worse. From financial to relationship issues to life challenges, there will be something that makes you feel there is a point of no return.

I have good news for you: I have been there and have risen to the top from it. This will be one of the hardest times in your life. You will want to give up, give in, quit, and feel there is a point of no return. Trust me when I say that I have felt it. Nothing can be worse. Are you feeling this way while you are reading this? I am sorry if you are, but I have good news for you: you are going to stop and start planning the action needed to rise to the top.

FOR AS LOW AS YOU FEEL, THAT DETERMINES THE HEIGHT OF YOUR SUCCESS.

I want you to start thinking you can do it. You can make it. You can get up and overcome those challenges, achieve those goals, and make the change needed in your life. Another essential element you need to make this happen, and I have talked about this in a previous chapter, is **faith**. I swear to you I have had miracles happen to me—things that can only be explained by having faith in God.

I will revert back to what I said before. You need the drive and dedication to make things happen, but you also need faith. During these hard times, the lows, the rejection, the questions, you must have faith that you will overcome this. I do not want to drift off too much into the spiritual world, but it is essential to success. Is there an ROI in God? You better believe it. I would not be writing this book or have accomplished what I have if it were not for God. How does this tie into business? I live by the simple motto:

WHATEVER YOU PUT OUT INTO THE WORLD IS WHAT YOU WILL GET IN RETURN.

Out of this whole book, one of the most important ingredients to your life and success is putting out positive energy. You may be saying that you have heard this a million times, but I am going to help break this down for you. You need to release your spirit and accept ANYTHING that can happen to you. It is literally a feeling of letting go of all your fears, doubts, and insecurities. Whether good or bad, you must let go of wondering what could happen to you.

The key is to stop asking "WHY?" Do not live your life and your decisions on the word "why." This will change your life in a heartbeat. Combine this with having faith, and you will start to see the changes. It may not happen overnight, but it will. Believe me, it will. I am sharing this with you is because this is not the typical way that people do business, see business or even live day to day. You hear almost every successful entrepreneur talk about the millions they have made, the cars they drive, the amount of companies they sold, etc. Well that is cool and all, but NO ONE talks about the spiritual side of success. Maybe they are afraid to talk about it, who knows, but I want to bring a new perspective into your life and not be the same "guru" that spams you with auto responders when you follow me or show off that I sold a company for millions. That is not what got me started in my business journey; what kicked things off were a miracle and some faith.

This was super important for me to get off my chest as I would not feel right if I did not share with you the keys to my success. And I assure you I am not a millionaire … yet. When they say the money will come, it is true. Do not think of the money, but focus on the story of how you got to that point. As important as it is to have 500,000 followers, it is even more important to have an actual story.

SUCCESS IN STORYTELLING

There are SO many overnight social-media success stories as well as broke college kids that work part time at a fast food restaurant, but then come home to put on their brand name outfits and make videos of themselves. These stories include girls that become famous from making makeup videos in their bathroom or guys with really nice hair making videos of them running their fingers through it. And somehow, they grow an audience. There are billions of people looking for this stuff on the Internet, which means that literally anyone can do something with their lives no matter how good or amateur it may be. You have loads of FREE platforms that allow you to create a name for yourself. The only difference between you and the kid living at home is that you have the opportunity to create a legacy and story for yourself.

Do not do something just for popularity as that WILL fade out. Do NOT start a business to be cool or because you have 20,000 followers. Do NOT attempt to partner with people JUST to gain exposure when they are doing what I described. It most likely will be short term, and it will be clear that you have no story. Your story is everything. It is what makes you relevant and authentic. That is what sells and what makes you who you are.

In 1999 when I created SalonSearch.com, the Internet was still a baby. Even I was unsure of what it really was until it clicked that this was the future. It was a new resource for people to find out information about pretty much anything they wanted. This was the perfect time to start something combining technology and beauty.

Let's take a step back for a second. Innovation is very important when you are starting a business. No one else was really doing this in the capacity that I was, or was so focused on a specific industry. I believe there was one for spas that came out shortly after; but having an idea, seeing the need and then executing it is the magic sauce. SalonSearch was an Internet directory of salons, which the consumer or client could use to search for a registered salon in their area. I know! Genius, right?

Well just to show how new the Internet was, people were mainly spending on newspaper ads. My strategy was to walk into salons or book an appointment with them to explain how the Internet was the new thing and why they HAD to be listed on my website. I was getting responses like: "I am afraid of the Internet." "I am not putting my information on the Internet." "What is the Internet? I will stick to newspaper ads." This was in 1999.

Now, if you do not put out your information or how people can find you somewhere online, you are almost cursed from growing any type of business. I was shocked how many people did not want to register. I had a pricing structure all set in place with different packaging options. It was affordable and much cheaper than the newspaper, but I really had no way to scale or show any return on investment on this. It was brand new.

I did not get ALL "No's." I had to give many away for free, but then I started to get paid listings! I will never forget my very first one. Of course, it was mostly made up of people I knew, but they still registered and paid me. I thought, "Holy crap, it's working!" I even took out newspaper ads myself to get the word out. Before I knew it, salons were calling ME to advertise and register. I could not believe that it was working! However, there is a huge part of this story that I have not mentioned, which is probably the most painful part of it all—development.

If you are starting a business or have an idea that you want to execute, you need to actually make it happen. How do you go about going from an idea to reality?

HERE IS THE FORMULA: IDEA + RESOURCES = BUSINESS

I was VERY lucky to have a close family friend named Kevin who happened to be a coder (programmer). I shared my idea with Kevin right from the start and till this day, I will never forget what he did for me. Kevin was working at an agency that had a business magazine. He knew everything about this platform from sales to coding. I told him I had no idea how to code and that I needed help to create this website. Now I had originally started this concept with an old high school friend, but I ended up breaking off the partnership several months later (still not sure if it was the right move but I needed to take this head on myself). I registered a new name for the site and then started from scratch.

Kevin and I talked about what I had accomplished previously and decided to build on that format. Kevin knew CFM (cold fusion markup) which was like the Holy Grail of database programming. You pretty much had to be like a genius to know it, and he was. We spent countless hours creating this site and setting up a platform to make it turnkey. From adding salons manually to what fields or information to display, it was all done by hand and came to life.

I was also learning the ins and outs of the IT world and the knowledge I obtained was invaluable. Till this day, I am so lucky to have experienced what I did back then. Kevin was kind enough to do this for me for free. He really helped me beyond belief. Not only did he help me from a technical perspective, but he also introduced me to "networking." You know, when you go to events to hand out your card and pitch your idea to everyone in the room.

The Internet was the new craze, and the number of people that had Internet businesses was unreal. Companies were selling Internet access! You had to actually pay companies to access the web just like we all do today with TV and phone plans. I know this all may sound prehistoric to you, but I feel knowing what I went through is very important to my story.

Again, it goes back to story. Even though I am in the beauty industry by trade, you could put me in a room of IT professionals and I could talk to them about coding and functionality for hours upon hours. I was learning the art of creating something. You must understand the ingredients needed to make YOUR idea a success. It takes resources—money, friends, ideas, planning, and dedication.

I hate to say this, but money is unfortunately what makes the world go round. If you are lucky enough to have friends to get you started that are willing to do it for free, that do not want ANYTHING from you, take them up on it—especially if they are like family.

After the site continued to grow, Kevin and I felt that it was too time consuming for him to manage my site as well as have a life of his own. So I decided to research web developers on the Internet. Turned out an old acquaintance of mine was a coder and worked for a local web design/marketing company. We set up a meeting and then BAM! I had my new programming company. I had NO idea what any of this stuff was going to cost, and back then, it was a free-for-all. The guys I worked with charged $85 per hour—and this was 1999. It sounded like a crap load of money, but companies like this one were just starting to take off so I agreed to do it. I had NO money. I was 24 years old.

Well I would not say any money, but I sure as heck did not have money for a start-up. So when I got my first bill of $14,000, I thought, "How the heck am I going to pay for this?" Oh wait! I have a credit card with like $30,000 credit and like no balance, so I got this. BIG MISTAKE. After redesigning the site two times with this company and an investment of about $70,000 that I did not have, SalonSearch was up and running and only making a LITTLE money. I owed about three times more to the coding company than I was making in earnings. The company ended up trying to overcharge me for something and we parted ways.

I do need to give credit to David, who was the owner of his company, for opening up my eyes to the world of business, marketing, design, and innovation. He was a Creative Director/ego maniac, but he did go out of his way and I did learn a lot from him and his team.

HANDS-ON EXPERIENCE

Much of business is learning out in the field. I feel like I learned more from my own business experiences than my college classes. If you are a young entrepreneur, you are going to think you know it all. Do you already feel that way? Go ahead then, it's fine. You will learn that you do not know it all. It is hard to brag that you are an entrepreneur unless you actually have started something, gone through the struggles and then built it up. Anyone can own or start a business these days. The struggles I went through would typically cause anyone to quit, which is why most people do not want to start a business. Persistence has been the best attribute I gained during my journey since I started. From starting my website in 1999, losing lots of money and the ups and downs—none of it has ever been a distraction for me. *Failure is not an option.*

The ability to sell yourself and share your story is really the most important asset in doing business. When someone reaches out to you without you having called them is when you know you are on the right track. How do you tell your story? Well you actually NEED to have one. Everyone is the best at what they do, right? You have a business for two days and you are the best of the best, right? LOL! It's like being a one-hit wonder or an overnight success if people cannot connect with YOU. Without connection, you have a long road ahead of you.

I cannot stress how crucial this is: focus on building your legacy and the story of how you got to where you are now. People need to know this, as it is all about relevance and authenticity. I can rattle off a list of accomplishments, struggles, challenges, and achievements to describe my brand—heck, that is why I am writing this book! If you are unsure of what your story is, then allow me to help you. This really is the backbone. List everything you have done in your life up to this point. Even if you make a bullet-point list and it is only comprised of two things, make the list anyway. Then, connect that with what you created, started, and built as a business. If you created a new pen, what is the story of why and how you got to the point of making one? Then, how did you actually make it? This is how you tell the story of you and your business.

When people approach me or I have to work with someone who has no story, I usually want to bail out after a few minutes. People will always try to sell you, but remember you have no obligation to buy from them. Remember that also when YOU are the one selling. No one HAS to do business with you. Sure, you can be an aggressive salesperson, but most people can smell that a mile away. Like Alec Baldwin said, "ABC. Always Be Closing!" You literally need to be on your A-Game 24/7. What you convey to people is a reflection of your brand. Trust me, it is. What is your likeability factor? Why should someone do business with you? You need to have all these questions answered in your story.

This whole book has been based off of storytelling. I want you to get to know who I am and what I have worked hard to do and why. My goal is to inspire you, make you laugh and educate you through my experiences as a person and entrepreneur. Make you laugh? Yes, it is who I am. I like to joke around and it is part of how I do business. Making people feel good is massive! You have to build a connection, earn trust, and raise the likeability factor. You have a better chance of doing business with someone who likes you trust me. Don't you hate a-holes? I do, too!

BACK TO MY STORY...

So let's bring things up to speed a little and get into how I built up what I did, how I make money from it and where I see things going. I started out just how Gary suggested: put a video camera in front of you, start filming, and do anything you can to get your name out there. Get in the public as much as you can and however you can. Keep in mind what I said earlier: you are a reflection of your own actions. If you put out crap, then it could harm you from the start.

I was actually told I should not do it—so I did. Remember to fuel the passion. I literally filmed myself doing videos to motivate people so I could build an audience. One by one people were watching and liking my content. I am not talking thousands of people. I am talking about 2–5 people a day! You MUST be patient when it comes to building up a brand. It does not happen overnight. It has taken me 6 ½ years to get to this point since 2010.

I then was given great advice, and I ran with it. I expanded my vision to a much broader and larger platform. I started networking more, putting myself out there. Things were starting to happen, but I had a short story to tell and something authentic. I was actually doing the work, which anyone could go online to see! Do NOT talk trash or hype yourself up in anyway if someone can Google your name and find NOTHING on you. It just makes you look bad. Do not call yourself a social media expert if you have no social profiles or hardly any followers. This WILL hurt you. Wait until you have built up something that you can reference—and that was what I was doing. It got me on TV, in magazines and on the radio. I went to events, walked Red Carpets, had my picture taken and all from building up from scratch.

At the first event I went to as an invited guest, I can recall like 20 people lined up to meet me and take pictures with me. Who am I to have all these people wanting to meet me? I was shocked, but overheard people saying, "That's The Salon Guy," then more people wanted to come meet me. It was crazy. You need to get out there to make yourself known.

A big lesson in that is you will waste a LOT of time going to events that are poorly run, unorganized, have all the same people, and really are just hot messes. I do suggest going through this period, as you will learn what NOT to do. So much of what I know is from the bad experiences. It builds character. Then, you will know what you need to do when it is your time to shine. My first event I threw for a web series I created drew over 800 people. I expected maybe 50–100. There was over an hour wait just to get in. I was overwhelmed by all the support from people.

Until now, I am still on the grind working pretty much seven days a week, all hours of the day. You have heard this a million times: time is money. I agree to an extent. Time is all you basically have, but you have plenty of it. So many people mismanage their time when it comes to most things in their lives. There are some great articles on how successful people manage their time. Some get up at 4:00 a.m.

and for the next 10–13 hours, all of their time is scheduled out with day-to-day tasks and routines. This works, trust me. Start organizing your time as if everything you do is like an appointment with yourself.

However, time does not always translate into money. Just because you put in five hours into a project, as an entrepreneur it does not mean you will earn for five hours of your time. Down the road, it may pan out that way, but not always immediately. The hardest thing for me was having patience and learning that the money will come. It is so easy to connect money with time, success and effort, but there is a thing called "sweat equity" that is just as valuable as cold, hard cash. This is a game that needs to be played out.

Most of the biggest names in business and entertainment say the money will come. You have to get in a state of mind where money is not the first thing on your agenda during the hustle phase. Yes, it is super important, and you need to be able to pay your bills, but this is why you properly manage your time and efforts.

Patience was another hard thing for me to grasp as I am super over-ambitious—so much so that I am my own worst enemy. I expect things to happen that day or the next. This was a hard lesson for me and things take time, especially in business.

How do you manage your day-to-day? Do you have small children? Work a full-time job? Do you feel like you have NO time to do anything besides your everyday responsibilities? Maybe starting a business is not for you. If it is, then you simply need to make sacrifices that will allow you to pave the road to getting things done. I am very lucky that my son will be in his 20s by the time this book comes out and does not need a babysitter. I have no other responsibilities in my life other than my own to survive.

It is very lonely doing what I do and expensive as well. There are huge rewards from a social media and public-eye standpoint, but as far as personal life, I gave much of it up many years ago. I am actually happy with my life and how things are currently. Most of my time is dedicated to growing my business, and that is awesome to me. Again, I can do this because I have the freedom and time to. These are choices and paths you can and need to take if you want to embark on this journey.

BLEEDING AND SWEATING FOR GOLD

Let's go back to the "blood, sweat, and tears" of business. When I say blood, I do not literally mean you will be bleeding or cause anyone to, but it is an expression that defines how far you will go to do what is needed for yourself. There have been scenarios where I may not have been bleeding; however, I do recall bleeding at times due to lugging around bags and backpacks. I have walked in pouring rain for 20 blocks, walked to destinations in freezing weather for long distances, had to wait around for 2+ hours just to get into an event—the list of tough experiences goes on and on.

Now here is where it gets interesting and this is where YOU can control the outcome of your painful scenarios. Will you want to give up? Yes. Will you be frustrated? Yes. Will you feel like you are getting nowhere? Yes. All of these emotions are something that my mentor taught me—and that is *normal*. These are all parts of the growing experience of discovering you, building your story, creating your character. The key is to *not* to expect anything, but to be *open* to anything happening.

It became very common for me to "predict" what was going to happen at an event or the outcome of me showing up somewhere that I did not want to go to, but once I learned how to release, yes a physical feeling of letting go, only good things came from my experiences. I stopped asking why, stopped having negative expectations, and stopped thinking I always knew what the outcome was going to be. I simply welcomed anything with an open heart and mind.

You have the ability to do this also and it will be life changing for both you and your career. Try this next time you go somewhere that may take a bit more effort than the normal scenario. Do not think of any outcomes, do not complain, and do not put any bad outcomes in your mind. Instead, think of only positive things coming your way and be open with *no* expectations. That is the most important part—*no expectations*. Simply be open and accepting from your heart and mind. I promise you, miracles will happen.

So many experiences that contribute to my success and story are not from investors or money or material things, but simply from being open. Let me tell you about the time I went to the *Today Show* in NYC. Miley Cyrus was performing live. I had to get up at 3:00 a.m. to take the first train at 4:30 a.m. to get to the NYC studio latest by 6:00 a.m. Little did I think that there would be any wait as I arrived at NBC studios outside, simply walked up to the front, and thought, "Wow that was easy; I'm early and no one is here yet."

I was then redirected to about three blocks down to see girls sleeping on the streets and literally hundreds and hundreds of people in line for blocks! I was telling myself that there was no way I was going to stand outside in freezing cold weather while it was still dark out with hundreds of people. Now before you start judging and asking why I wanted to see Miley Cyrus live as a straight, 40-year-old man, it was because I wanted to see how she connected with her audience. See what she did with her fans; how she treated them; how they treated her; and what were the interactions like. I wanted to soak it all up from the biggest pop star at that time. She was the most talked about person in the media as she just hosted the MTV Video Music Awards.

So off I went. Instead of being mad and frustrated, I decided to release those emotions and just accept whatever happened. Before I knew it, the line started moving and was then split up based on how many people were in a group. I said I was alone so I got moved up way past many others. Suddenly, I was in and could hear Miley doing her warm up. This was for the summer concert series, but it was very cold at 5:00 to 6:00 a.m. My spot was kind of far from the stage. There were already at least 100 people standing near the stage so they must have been there all night waiting. Miley's live performance on the *Today Show* was minutes away and I was ready to go. I thought to myself that I should have been closer or something special was going to happen, but I just was not sure what it was. I felt it though, but had no expectations.

One of the security guards asked if I was alone and I said yes. Thankfully, he bumped me up to be three rows back from her and I thought that was the first good thing to come. It was amazing to see her fans and hear her engage with them during the commercial breaks. She asked who was going to buy her new album that was coming out the next day and like 300 people were screaming, "Meeee, meeeee, meeeee!" I was blown away that someone could have such an influence over people. Then it hit me—she is selling herself just like anyone else would. The amount of people that screamed yes to buying her album translated into like hundreds of thousands of dollars just from one sentence.

An employee from the show was telling people to send Tweets in for Miley. So I sent one out not really expecting anything, but once again, I felt something good was going to happen, with no expectations. I was simply open to it. So I sent out my Tweet and there it went into the universe. Miley was on her last song and I remember seeing her pointing to the camera singing her last group of lyrics. She was done and the segment was over. I stood there amongst hundreds of screaming fans and was thinking what a great experience it was. I suddenly got a text message, then a few messages on Facebook telling me how they saw TheSalonGuy across their TV screens. I was confused because I did not know how that was possible in such a massive crowd.

I got back home, jumped online, and found the performance videos on YouTube. Yes, four hours later they were up online. So I watched the first segment. Then the second song and then I said to myself, "LOOK, there I am!" I saw myself in the shots where I was standing after I got moved closer. I assumed that was what everyone meant when they said they saw me. Miley was singing her last song. Remember when I said that she was singing her last lyrics into the camera? And how I was open for anything to happen? As she was singing into the camera, my Tweet popped up on TV to her and the *Today Show* and was held there for a good 5–6 seconds as she ended her performance.

I started to tear up. No not because of "fan-girling" over Miley, but because this was the miracle that I left myself open to experiencing. I took a screen shot of the moment my Tweet came up and it was like she was looking right at me, pointing to me. It may not be a big deal to some, but after getting up at 3:00 a.m., standing outside for over an hour, freezing, being surrounded by screaming teens, and feeling awkward, it was a big deal for me and will be a part of my story forever. What you put in, you will get in return if you open yourself up to it. Make the sacrifices, take chances and take risks. You WILL get results.

Did I earn money from that? No. But that moment will be a part of my presentations when I speak to groups and will always be part of my journey to success. Many of the things that have happened to me most likely will never happen again. They are very special and rare. Hold those very close to you and be proud of what you did to earn it.

That is not the only story like that. At least 5–10 more things of that rare nature happened to me. They will to you as well if you believe. I really hope I am painting a clear picture for you of the type of person I am and how what I have accomplished can be done by anyone who wants it. For years and years, I felt like there was no end to hard work, no results, and no success. My life has been a long journey, and I am just at the middle stage of it all. Not giving up after a week is cool, but try 20+ years of not giving up and working hard based off of your passion and drive.

Did I make money along the way? Sure I did. It was not like I was broke. In fact, I was probably earning about $1,000 cash a week for the early part of my 20s. I worked two jobs, but I was a hustler. I wish I knew more about money back then or was given guidance. I would have so much money now if I had been smarter. The important part though is that I was earning money. It is great to have goals and to want to be successful, but you NEED to survive. Please be realistic with your goals and desires. I play golf, and I am a decent golfer. I was down to a six handicap in my early 20s. Was I good enough to be a pro or play on tour? No. I played in local tournaments and loved playing, and even toyed with going to school to be a pro, but I realized it was just a hobby for me. Even people that shoot under par have a small chance of even making a career out of it. I was realistic and gave up the idea of wasting years and years on wanting to become a pro.

By all means, do not let what I am saying discourage you from following your dreams, but it is crucial to be very realistic with what you are doing and how far you can take it. Also realize how you can make a living from it. That is probably the most important part. I see so many people spend countless amounts of time, weeks, months, years sticking to something thinking they will be successful from it, then to realize they have been broke all along and then try to jump into a different career later in life. All of these things are okay, and it is part of your journey. However, if I can help bring you down to reality and help save you time, money, and effort, then I am happy to do so.

You *have* to make money while you are growing your passion or starting off in life as a young adult. Mom and Dad cannot keep paying for everything. I wish I was financially independent at an early age and was not so spoiled. I am grateful for it, but the last thing I want is for my son to be 40, living at home with no money. I went through tough times in my life and it makes me so frustrated knowing the solution to all of it was getting good advice. I was somewhat of a rebel, which did not help much, but man do I wish I had done things differently.

Let's get back on track with "the-how" part of this story. I am by no means rich financially, but I am rich in knowledge, and much of that is priceless. Well actually, I DO put a price on it—and it is what I charge for what I do, in other words, my worth. What is your time worth? What are you charging for your work? Remember how I said do not think of the money? When it comes to your actual passion and goals do not think, just do. Have your side job that you can earn money from and hopefully enjoy. However, as a new entrepreneur you will likely end up working for free, volunteering your time, getting low-paid gigs and feeling sometimes like you are not getting anywhere. Those experiences are normal. You have to put in the labor and sweat equity. Experience, or in gaming we say XP, is everything. Once you have enough experience, THEN you can start putting a price tag on it.

I find it somewhat frustrating when someone with 500 followers on social media boasts that they are social-media experts. Or the guy who is a network marketer who wrote three e-books and does nothing but spam you about his millions—that is not the way to do business in my eyes. If anything, it causes me to NOT want to do business with you. If you have no story or if your success is not obvious or transparent about how you got there, then there is no way I am doing business with you or even talking to you. Your price tag comes from earning it through all of your XP. Everyone wants or has a price tag associated with his or her business. There is no real math on how to get that number in my opinion, but rather a simple equation that will add up to what you can charge based on your worth.

Can you come right out of college and charge $100 an hour for a service? Not likely, but that hourly rate has to be determined by all of the experience, education, and expertise you have obtained over the years. Be fair, but know your value. What can you bring to the table to a potential client or customer? Remember, no one HAS to do business with you. It is your opportunity to sell yourself to anyone, but do not *expect* them to do business with you.

How do you sell yourself? My best method of selling myself is simply by being me: honest, nice, and knowledgeable. You must also have some form of credibility under your belt that you can sell. People will only trust you if you can show high-profile accomplishments.

How this all ties into your business is the core foundation of how you build it. Hard work, sacrifice, commitment, dedication, and mostly faith are what it takes. It is easy to have sold a company for millions or to have been brought into it as you got older. I take that back, it is not easy to sell a company, but money gives you the opportunities to make your dreams come true and to have the resources to make it happen. I literally started with little to no money. My first business in 1999 was funded by credit cards, which was the worst thing I could have done, but it was all I had. Now, there are many resources available to you for funding.

Do you need start-up cash? Perhaps, but you can also build something from nothing. It takes NO money to start a YouTube channel. You actually invest normal money into it. Normal money is what I call essentials that you are spending on anyways. You can film from a cell phone, get Internet access, and edit from a laptop or tablet, or start a blog for under $30 a month or even for free. You really can start with an idea, some passion, and the desire to succeed. I know you want to make money right away, and this is not going to happen sorry to say. I spent almost two years making little to no money with my brand. Most of my time was spent building up my credentials and sweat equity. Walking all over the streets of NYC to go to an event, getting up at 3:00 a.m. to jump on an opportunity, or going to events to get denied and turned down for something. The amount of time I invested in myself was painful, but necessary. I would not be here nor have the knowledge I do if it was not for all that hard work I put in.

When I tell you it was hard, I mean it. Even till this day, there are points of discouragement, depression, and even loss of hope, but then I smack myself in the head and tell myself that **failure is not an option**. I have no time to fail or give up. My hard work will pay off. I remember walking to an event in NYC in freezing-cold weather, and I was so frustrated. I kept asking myself, is all of this effort worth it? I was all dressed up in a nice suit, carrying a camera bag and feeling full of doubt. I then told myself that I had to be patient and not to expect anything right away. Good things would come in due time.

You must have patience when it comes to your success. I am a super overly ambitious person and I had to train myself to be more patient and to understand that things do not always happen over-night. It has taken me over six years to get to this point and that is after being in my industry for over 20 years! You have to be in it for the long run. SO many people these days are in it short term or want the over-night success story, but in my opinion that will only last for so long.

Let's talk about how you can actually make money now. This whole book is designed to inspire and motivate you, but in the end, building a brand or business is about selling and making money. This is the hardest part of any start-up because you do not always see the return right away. It could take a few years before you see any true profit. Setting up an action plan is one way to simplify it even more.

Look at what you are selling, how much you would pay for it, and then how you are going to sell it. I had no idea how I was going to make money at the start, and even to this day, I am always working on new services to offer.

Let's look at what you are actually selling. Are you selling products or services? Whatever it is you are selling, please, please, please be fully aware of what you are getting into, your target audience, and your competition. Chances are there is someone else that is trying to do the same thing. The biggest difference is what and how you are doing it differently than the next person.

Let's go back in time to when I first launched my YouTube channel. There was virtually no one really putting hair-related videos out there in the way I was doing it. I had a mission right from the start to inspire people and to build TheSalonGuy brand. From that point on, it was full steam ahead. NOTHING was going to stop me or get in my way. **Failure is not an option**. I still have the same attitude and drive today that I did over six-plus years ago. If anything, it is much stronger now since realizing results.

Now there are hundreds if not thousands of people putting hair/beauty-related content on the Internet. It is very easy to get discouraged by seeing what others are doing, but what you have to do is **focus** on your own stuff and only compete with yourself. Do NOT copy what others are doing or try to replicate other brands to the point to where it is clear that you are copying. Instead, create "you" and determine how you want to get your point across.

I have always loved comedy so I always incorporate some form of comedy or humor into what I do. Be yourself and build up what you believe in. I have spent countless hours watching motivational videos, listening to audio books, reading magazines and books, attending seminars and doing whatever it was I could to understand the business. I wanted to identify a direction and understand the media itself.

Putting yourself out there is the biggest part of growing a brand. For anyone who knows me and has asked me for advice, I have always said you need to put yourself out there. You reflect your brand. If you are a hot mess, drama queen or super unprofessional, your business and brand will best be known for those characteristics.

There are things that I may do in my personal life that I would not necessarily bring to the table in business. I am able to separate the two, and you must be able to know how to act and when. At the start, I was very insecure being in front of a camera. I did not have a full head of hair nor look like Ryan Seacrest, but over time, I started to change the way I thought and made the focus less on me and more on the viewer. This is key when it comes to selling yourself.

Stop making it all about YOU and make it more about the viewer or customer. They are the ones who will be purchasing from you and supporting you so make them the priority. You are fulfilling a specific need they have—be it a tutorial on makeup or one on how to edit photos. The content you put out is meant to inspire, educate, or motivate. Whatever you sell will only be sold if you act authentically, become transparent, and be yourself.

People can smell an aggressive or shady salesperson a mile away. It is amazing how many people still use the 1985 way of selling. In fact, I was getting gas the other day and there was a guy in front of me in a tinted minivan. He got out of his car to complain about how warm it was and took off his jacket. While he was complaining, he was trying to make eye contact with me to engage me in some way. I did not make much of it nor did I interact with him beyond a smirk, but I could smell something fishy by the way he was being aggressive. He was done getting gas and then proceeded to drive his minivan next to me at the gas pump and asked me if I needed a theatre system or a projector. Remember I said that one of my many jobs when I was younger was selling speakers out of a van? That was 1993. I tried it for one day. I told the guy in the van that I was not interested and that I used to do the same thing he was doing when I was younger. He got very defensive and nasty then drove off saying, "Yeah, what happened?" as if I was missing out on a career. Do not get me wrong, if you need to sell to make a living then do it, but please do not be one of those guys. You need to have tact and be cool.

I spent almost two years making little to no money with TheSalonGuy because I was building up my name, reputation, and credibility. I had a lot to sell and offer in my mind, but I did not have much experience to back it up. That time frame is enough to cause anyone to give up. It is normal to want to give up, loose hope or become discouraged. I used to feel so alone and like I was the only other person who felt this way until one of my mentors shared that it was completely normal. This helped relieve much of my stress and made me realize it is a part of being an entrepreneur. From that point on, I just accepted that it was all a part of growing and just pushed through it.

The main part of this journey is to **NOT GIVE UP**. So many people make it to a point where they give up when they were so close to going to the next level. I like to describe this as breaking through the wall. Once you break through that barrier, it is a whole different experience. It is like going from the minors to the major league. It becomes a whole new playing field. Keep in mind you are now dealing with better players also.

Before you break through, you must go through the experiences necessary to actually get through. This includes doing stuff for free, doing things that you might feel waste time, or getting an education on what you need to learn. I encourage you to watch videos, read magazines and books, and other tools that are essential to your growth. You may end up getting rejected from a gig you hoped to land, being denied access to that event you hoped to get into, or trusting someone who turns out to be a complete waste of time and resources. The list of bullshit goes on and on—and trust me, I have seen it all. Once you go through all of that and have a clear vision of what you are selling, then you will be ready to break through the wall. After you do, there is no turning back.

From here on out is where you have to think of yourself as a business, a brand. You actually should from the start, but remember what I said about having to put the time in. Now that you have pushed through, it is business time. Here is where you can start to charge for your services and feel fully confident about it. The hard part is that you will still end up offering stuff for free, bartering, and doing the stuff you did when you first started. That hardly ever goes away, but when you firmly put out to the world that it is all about business now, then you will see the biggest change.

At this stage in the game, I have a number of ways that I earn my money: my hair products, YouTube, videos and marketing services, and doing hair. Surprisingly, after putting in 20+ years in as a stylist, doing hair is what brings in the least amount of money for me on paper. Why do I still do it? I love my clients and having my hands in it really keeps me relevant and up to par with my skills. I do, however, know many stylists who just do editorial work and do not work on clients anymore. We shall see what the future holds for me, but for now, I am sticking with it. There are plenty of days that I just do not want to cut hair anymore, plenty of times where I want to just walk away from it all, but I am realistic with myself about what I am best at doing. Then I change my mindset on what I can do to be happier.

Writing this book is a huge step in my brand and career. See what patience and faith will do for you? There was a time not too long ago where I was pretty much on the verge of being broke. Yes, broke. I had to sell almost all of my most treasured items that I had over the years from records, DJ equipment, sports gear, and much more. I was not homeless, but I had faith and needed to push through the hard times and believe that if I kept working, something good would come from it. The one thing that really helped me out in the lowest time in my life financially was the sale of my childhood house where I lived with my Mother Josephine and my sister. The money was split four ways and the amount I received, which was somewhat small, helped me pay off debts and invest in my business.

What is amazing, however, is how fast money can go. There was a point when I had over $80,000 in my bank account. Within seven months, more than three-quarters was already gone. Granted, I used the money to pay off debts and invest in myself, but it was a miracle that it happened when it did. That is how life works. You never know when something is going to happen. You need to have faith and be patient. Do not *expect* anything just be open to it.

Since I launched my products in September 2015, I have pretty much made my investment back. However, I am now spending a lot just to keep up with the orders. I have the problem most entrepreneurs want when they start. I have learned though, that many businesses will fail due to not having the money for growth. Who knows, maybe some nice investor will come along? *Failure is not an option* for me so I am going to keep growing my brand and business to the best of my ability.

I would be lying if I told you there were no days that I wanted to just walk away. I often think of the amount of money I would have saved up if I DID NOT invest or spend all of it. Heck, I would have been driving a Porsche by 25 and owning my own house, but this is the path I chose and I cannot control the outcome. At least I got to write a book about it, right?

CHAPTER 7

MENTORS AND PEOPLE

A **LOT OF THINGS WOULD NOT HAVE HAPPENED IF IT WERE NOT** for certain people that helped change my life. This chapter will be somewhat short, but I want to share a few stories on how I connected with these influential people. I could mention many people in this chapter, but I am going to focus on those people I have met in the last few years and how these experiences relate to business.

I did not talk much about my son earlier in the book because I wanted to save him for this chapter. I was 20 years old and in a relationship with his mother, who was 19 when she became pregnant. It was the typical story of her being late for her period. We started to panic and had a strong feeling she was pregnant. I think my mother put the baby spell on us as she used to yell at me for spending too much time with his mother doing you know what every five minutes. Well, her "spell" worked as we confirmed she was pregnant when she took a pregnancy test.

At first, we both freaked out, but then within minutes we were celebrating. We were very much in love and felt we were going to be together so we wanted to make it work. I started to get a bit overwhelmed with the bigger picture of this situation and reality set in. I was only 20, how was I supposed to raise a child? After telling my family, and even going to my family doctor, I was advised she should get an abortion, which really hurt me. I was told I was too young and there was no way I could raise a child. I did not want to have an abortion because I wanted to be the father I never had—and this was very deep and meaningful to me.

I sought the advice of a priest who gave me a few resources to call. The information provided helped me realize that it was possible to raise a child. I discovered there were financial programs available for young people like myself in this situation. After conducting all of the research and doing what I could to ensure my son could come into this world and be raised properly, I stuck with my decision to have him. His mother and I were in agreement as well, and till this day, he is a blessing to me. His birth was a true miracle as I grew up without a father. He was my opportunity to be one.

My son is a very special person to me and I honestly miss him being a baby. He was so cute and laid back. As he grew up, he brought so much joy to me. Seeing him also become a young man is truly a blessing. All you parents out there understand the challenges of having a 20-something-year-old child. Regardless of the ups and downs, he will always be my miracle and "game-changer."

The next person I want to talk about is Ben. About four or so years ago, I was blessed to meet a guy named Ben from California. I discovered him on YouTube in a motivational video he did for a beauty school sharing how he lost over 90 pounds with his own methods, which led him to write a few books about it. There was something about him that really resonated with me. He basically told it like it was—no BS, just straight up good information delivered in an inspiring way.

I simply reached out to him and we began to exchange emails. He was awesome, and before long, we were talking on the phone. I shared my journey and mission on growing my brand. We both became very inspired by each other and created a great friendship. I call him my guardian angel.

The story I wanted to share about Ben and how God works in ways we cannot understand is when I had the chance to cover The Oscars for the first time. At that point, I barely knew Ben and my biggest focus at that time was getting approved by The Oscars. I was on edge waiting to hear back from them, but then I finally got the email confirmation that I was approved! This approval was one of my biggest accomplishments; I was ecstatic. Then reality set in that I hardly had any money, no place to stay, and pretty much no way of getting there.

I became very depressed and pretty much gave up all hope of getting there. I remember going to sleep very upset. Later that evening I woke up crying. It must have been around 3:00 a.m. and I swear I got a sign from Mary, as I can recall seeing a bright light. I had a feeling of calmness and like I would never have to feel a worry in my life ever again. The weird part was that I woke up in tears, trembling with my heart racing. I definitely felt it was something very powerful, but I did not know whom to talk to so I called Ben. I shared this experience with him, and he said that it sounded like a sign from the Holy Spirit. I had never experienced that before.

Ben acknowledged he thought it was a sign and asked what troubled me. I admitted to him that I could not afford to go to The Oscars, as I did not have the money for the hotel stay, flight, and expenses. Then he told me that he had a spare bedroom I could stay in, a car I could drive, and basically said my place was his place. All of my fears, stress, and worries instantly went away. Ben has always been there for me and truly knows me as a person better than pretty much anyone. I am still in touch with him and consider him a great friend.

> *"Stephen is my inspiration. He is proof that someone can be humble and successful at personal branding without getting an ego about it. The first time we talked, it was like we had grown up together and known each other all our lives. What I wish more people knew about Stephen is that he is always thinking of how he can be there for others. This is a guy who was a volunteer police officer and fireman. He was a foster child, if you can believe it, and he was so loveable that his mother adopted only him out of about 80 children she housed throughout the years.*
>
> *Stephen measures his success in whether he can connect with just one person no matter if it is business or*

life. People seem to pick up on that because he is like a magnet for happiness and smiles. At Oscar week, I was so impressed at how Stephen was the exact same guy no matter who was near him. He was just as warm and genuinely interested in what strangers had to say as the A-Listers he interviewed. Whether on or off camera, you get the same Stephen Marinaro. That's my brother, right there. We have a million dumb inside jokes that make us crack up even if other people think we are dorky. We always talk about hustle but he has never expressed any desire for riches or fame in all the years I have known him. He really just wants a front row seat to cheer other people onward to their dreams. Losing his mother was a permanent wake-up call to Stephen. He knows life is precious and short so he makes every minute a labor of love.

Here's a quick story about Stephen that encapsulates what kind of guy he is. A few years back, we were at a gas station in Hollywood filling up my used Volkswagen with gas. Stephen tried to pay for my car and pump the gas for me but I wouldn't let him do it. We were chatting about whatever and this ridiculous car pulled up. We looked it up on our phones later and saw it was more than $110,000 for the car. This gorgeous young woman got out, dressed to the nines. She was one of the most beautiful women on the planet and happened to be a bona fide celebrity overseas as an A-list foreign pop star, although we did not know that until later. Anyhow, she was on the other side of the pump and no part of me even considered talking to her because she seemed so elite. Out of the blue, she struck up a friendly conversation with Stephen. They chatted it up and Stephen was talking with her just the same as any of the other hundreds of people he had already met in the last few days of Oscar week.

Within five minutes, she opened up with stories, being totally genuine with him as though they had been friends for years. In this situation, a lot of guys would probably try to flirt or get her phone number but there was never any hint of that kind of energy with Stephen. He was just a good listener, fully present for what she was saying. She gave him some contact info and the whole interaction was warm and professional. Stephen was completely cool and unaffected by the whole thing. When we got in the car, I looked up her info and saw that she was very famous abroad. Stephen seemed to look right past all of that and just saw her as a regular person. He said it was really hard to break into her industry and that showed hard work and dedication on her part. He had so much respect for that work ethic and her self-discipline. He was happy to see nice people succeed. I was waiting for him to make a comment about her looks because she was obviously drop-dead gorgeous but the conversation never went there. We just trailed off and talked about how much we liked hard work, or "hustle," as Stephen likes to call it.

I bring up that story because I am still impressed at how Stephen was not tempted by her beauty, wealth, or success. He is the same cool, relaxed guy no matter who is around him. He really just loves people and has a real gift for making it cool to be yourself. Stephen has been the catalyst for so many good things in my personal life and business. I am so proud of how he has found the strength to keep making videos, launching products, taking risks with good backup plans in place, and working hard no matter what. I absolutely love Stephen, as you can tell, and he is one of my closest friends. Above all, he's just a great guy."

—Benjamin Theisen

Next, we have Anthony. Like most of the mentors in my life, I discovered them through some sort of media such as a book or a YouTube video. I saw Anthony on YouTube doing a speech on business, motivation, and sales. He had a method that has pretty much made him famous and led to him writing a few books. After watching a few of his videos, I felt that I needed to reach out to him. This was still very early on in the game, but I was starting to make some progress and was experiencing the normal challenges that entrepreneurs face.

His website was listed in his video description and I found his email. I sent him an email with a short story explaining how I needed some help and felt lost in growing my business. Within 10 minutes, he replied back to me saying that he was free at that very moment to talk for a few minutes. I almost fainted when he said to call him. I called him and spent about 10 minutes on the phone with him. Before I called, I grabbed a pen and pad because I sure as heck was going to take notes on anything he advised me. After 10 minutes of talking and about five pages worth of notes, he shared that he had to go as he was giving a speech the next day at 9:00 a.m., but I could call him at 7:00 a.m. if I wanted to continue.

I went to bed so overwhelmed and in shock that I even got to talk to him. Just to give you an idea, he is worth millions and gets about $15,000 on average to give a speech. I had set my alarm clock for 6:45 a.m. The alarm went off and I sat up thinking to myself, one I am tired as hell and two, there is no way I am going to bother this guy at 7:00 a.m. It was 6:59 and I had made up my mind that I was just going to go back to bed. Suddenly, I got a slap in the head by my inner self. It said if someone who is worth millions of dollars and who is a huge success tells me to call him at 7:00 a.m, I need to frigging call him at 7:00 a.m.

At 7:01 a.m. I called him. He answered and his first response was, "So what did you think about our talk last night?" I could not believe that he remembered and was actually not hanging up on me. So we picked up where we left off and I admitted to him that I was not going to call. Here is the main moral to the story. He shared that about 90 percent of people DO NOT make the call. Making the effort and dedication to call and prepare for our talk proved to him that I was already on the road to success. That was pretty much life changing and will always be a part of my story. Anthony has gone on to help me in many of my decisions and still is a mentor to me.

Gary Vaynerchuk—I discovered Gary on YouTube while searching for motivational speeches. I came across a keynote video of him talking about doing what you love and how you can make a living from it. I then learned that he had a book called *Crush It*. I purchased the book and it literally jumpstarted my path to becoming a brand and creating a business based around what I love. I followed the steps he laid out pretty much to a tee, and before long, I had become a huge fan and considered him a role model.

I made it a goal of mine to meet him. It took almost a year and a half for him to engage with me. Not only did I get to shake his hand, I formed a relationship with him where I could reach out to him and he would respond. He is a great source of inspiration and has a no-BS approach to business, and that is what I respect about him.

These people have had a direct impact on growing my business and creating the brand I work so hard on. My family, friends, and countless people I have met over the years have all been an inspiration to me in some regard, and I am truly grateful for everything I have learned from them.

CHAPTER 8

THE TAKEAWAY

IN THIS FINAL CHAPTER, I WANTED TO PROVIDE SOME OF THE MOST important lessons I have learned in life and business. This chapter alone could be its own book, but I feel if you could only take away one chapter, this would be it. I wanted to tell you my story so that you have a better understanding of the person I am, and I hope you felt a connection with me. Too many people these days are becoming famous because of their looks or some controversial publicity stunt. I simply have been working hard, building from the ground up. So let's get into the key points.

» Always be polite.

» Treat others as you wish to be treated.

» Do not expect anything in life; instead, be thankful for what comes your way, as we do not have control of our destiny. Be thankful and accept what happens in your life as it is meant to be, good or bad.

» Do not ask, "Why?" I used to ask why all the time and I just kept making things more difficult on myself. Now I just thank God for the end result.

» Whatever you put out into the world will come back to you. Your life and actions will be a mirror image so what you put out you will get back in return. Think about this from relationships to jobs. If all you post on social media is pictures of your boobs, guess what type of attention you will get in return.

» STOP posting nothing but drama on social media. You are literally setting yourself up to receive it all back in your life. What you put out into the world will come right back to you. The more you publicly share all of your issues, drama, and struggles, that is what your life will consist of. Try to resist from sharing anything that is negative for a whole week and I promise you that you will be shocked how many good things will happen to you.

» You are whom you hang around. If you hang around people that want to party five nights a week, that will dramatically impact your life.

» Do not be cheap. Always offer some form of gratitude and efforts to pitch in, regardless of what it is.

» Do not wait for opportunities to come knocking at your door. They will only knock if you make an effort in the first place.

» Work harder AND smarter.

» Learn as much as you can about as much as you can. The more you know, the more interesting you are and you will be able to adapt to many more situations and environments.

» Do something to give back.

» Be selfish when it comes to your business and life. You will need to make sacrifices in order to grow and build your business. It is painful to hear, and I used to feel guilty, but now I do not let anything get in the way of my hard work and dedication to my path and goals. It will be hard for some people to grasp, but that is usually because they do not have a business or have no idea what it is like to start one.

» Detach yourself from places, people, or things that do not complement or support your vision or lifestyle. Do not intentionally hurt anyone, but cut people loose that simply bring you down.

» When starting a company and a brand, be authentic and organic. Do not buy views, likes, followers, or do anything un-natural to grow your brand as it will simply come back to bite you in the ass at some point.

» Do not spam your business info or posts on other people's social media pages. It is the worst thing you can do especially when starting out. I learned this the hard way. (Thanks Ryan Biddulph for the tip many years ago.)

» If you have an idea, a passion, or a love for something, just do it. You can start a business from it or simply enjoy it as a hobby.

» Understand the difference between being passionate for something and being realistic. There is a huge difference. Many "hipster-preneurs" are selling "passion" as the almighty must-have in order to start a business. So yes, you need to have passion, but you need to be realistic with yourself when it comes to whether you can do this for a living or not.

» If you are unsure of what you want to do in life, follow this formula. Write out a list of all your hobbies and interests. It can be 3, 5, 10, or 100 things. Next, make a second list where you take the things you can see yourself realistically doing and write those down. From that list, narrow it down to two things you can really see yourself doing after you think about it and do some research on where it can take you in life. Lastly, do ALL the research you can on those two passions you have from how much you can make, to opportunities, to benefits, to your ultimate happiness.

Then, write down that ONE thing that is clear to you and that is what you should do.

» Pray every day.

» Eat healthy and exercise.

» Get up early, as you can get more stuff done that way.

» Always show up early.

» Never be late.

» Communication is key. In your personal life as well as your professional life.

» Answer emails that are important to you.

» Do not ever let someone bring you down.

» You are not responsible for other people's issues especially if you have nothing to do with them or why they are there in the first place. Break away from people or relationships that are full of drama and especially when they blame you or weigh you down. Those types of people will blame you for their own bullshit and it is not fair to you. Trust me, RUN AWAY.

» Do not ever be jobless. Earning some money is better than no money.

» Become independent as early as you can in life.

» Start saving money as soon as you start earning it. Trust me, you will be thanking me in the future.

» Bail out of a situation that you feel is not right.

» Always go with your gut.

» Pray for the answer and it will come to you.

» Set standards in your life.

» Be the brand you want to be. Remember that you are your own representation of your brand so your actions are very important.

» Love yourself more.

» Find mentors and people you can look up to. This is very important because you will feel lost and alone.

» Do not follow advice from people that do not know what you do or how to do it. Everyone and their cat will give you advice and expect you to follow it, especially family. Listen to them when it is relevant to what YOU do and how it connects with your life. Do not feel pressured—ever—by anyone unless they are or have done the same as you have.

» Lastly, indulge every once and a while. Do something alone that is rewarding, fun, and an escape from all the stress and hard work you dedicate yourself to each day.

CONCLUSION

I sincerely thank you for reading this book. My wish is that there was something that inspired you in this book that will push you to make a change, work harder, or realize if I can do it, so can you. Most of success comes from hard work and simply doing it. There are so many scientific theories and formulas that modern entrepreneurs come up with and create 15-page charts that try to explain how to make a sale, but in my opinion, it is much easier than that. Just do it. Work harder, be nice to people, and treat them how you want to be treated. That alone is much more of a driving force than reading 50 pages on how to sell something. I am old school. I believe in the people and communication aspect of business, life, and gratitude. Offer a service or a product that people need, and do it in a classy and proper way.

Life will throw curveballs at you constantly. There will be plenty of times where you feel like giving up, feel like you are alone, or feel pressures of life, family, work or loved ones that you just want to escape from. Well, it is ok to escape. It is alright to feel how you feel. We cannot control what life has in store for us, so just accept it. Remember when I said to stop asking why? The moments when you want to ask, that is when you need to give thanks instead and realize some things are out of your control. What *is* in your control, however, is who you hang around, where you work, what you choose to do in life, how hard you work, and how you treat people. We have total control over many things in our lives, so stop complaining if you are waiting around for something to happen. Go out there and DO IT. The only person stopping you is you most of the time. If money is an issue, think of what you can do and how you can do it for little to no money. You can literally start a business off your cell phone. It just requires dedication and commitment. Trust me and promise me you will do it.

This book has been a true blessing in my life, and I hope to change lives by sharing my story and how anyone has the ability to make huge life accomplishments. I was also very realistic and fortunate to find a specific niche. Find your niche, and do it. Follow the formula I shared on what it is you should be doing. A book was a dream of mine many years ago. I actually started to write one but put it aside with no intentions of actually releasing it. This was truly a gift and message from God that I had to share my story with the world. The biggest question I learned is, "How do you want to be remembered?" How do you want people to remember you? I often ask this question when I do keynote speeches and it always results in people just going into a deep state of thought. It is a very intense question and one you should ask yourself often. How do you want to be remembered?

I want to be remembered for inspiring people, helping people, and being a hard worker. I love to make people laugh so I want to be remembered for being funny. Making people laugh is a great feeling. Usually my jokes take a few minutes to kick in or what I like to call it: long-term laughter. You won't laugh now but you will in say 10 minutes. I kindly ask that you remember me. I sincerely thank you for taking the time to read about my life, my story, and the ups and downs I have experienced.

A huge thank you to my family and friends for being there for me, inspiring me, and believing in me. The people I mentioned in this book as well as the many people I have encountered, I thank you. There are many people that I am no longer in contact with simply because I have become somewhat of a loner, and it takes that sometimes when building a business, but I have learned so much from so many people. I am fortunate to have had so much support in the beginning when I first started, and I will never forget each person who was there for me.

May all your dreams come true. Love more, eat better, exercise more, work harder, and treat others as you wish to be treated.

I do not know what my future holds, but I do have a dream to be on talk shows and being interviewed about this book. I want to help the world and especially people in business to focus more on the spiritual side of things. The emotional side of business and the stuff hardly anyone talks about. Is another book in the works? Not sure where this will take me, but it has been a true pleasure writing it. Once again, thank you for reading it.

SIDE STUFF

Writing this book has been extremely hard. I had a year to write this and I thought it was going to be much easier. I did not want to hire a ghostwriter, and many people suggested I hire one. I wanted to be authentic and true to my own words. I felt I could write it best. Of course, the editing process will be a big part of it, but I did not want anyone else to write this book except me.

I am friends with other authors, and I asked them all for advice on how to write, when to write, and the various outcomes that could happen from writing a book. I feel this is a great addition to my brand as it is a part of my growth. I am now sharing my story and how I got where I am. It has been an emotional journey filled with success stories as well as challenges. I do not wish any hard times on anyone, but at the same time success comes from failure and struggles. Sure, it is great to inherit millions of dollars or to sell a company and be instantly rich, but that is not going to happen for everyone. I feel I am only just breaking ground. And that is after a good 20+ years of working in a professional environment and even changing careers at some point. Most people want to be successful in a week!

Someone recently asked me what was the tipping point and when things started to turn a new leaf for my life and business. The moment happened when I was on national TV. When you work so hard and then have the opportunity to get seen by millions of people, it legitimizes you as a person and a brand. The key is that I was not a one-hit wonder and I was already building up a brand/business. Many people get lucky because they can fill the role of what is needed for a TV show and that may end up being very temporary. What it did for me was propel my name and brand forward, which I have not given up on.

Being able to have credentials is beyond important. There is a lot of BS going on out there, but if you have the credibility to back it up then you are on the right path. Do not promote yourself as a social-media expert if you hardly have any followers or call yourself a YouTube expert with only 1,000 subscribers. You need the experience and credentials to back it up, trust me.

One of the hardest situations in my life was being 20 years old and knowing I was going to be a father. I kept it a secret from everyone at my job because I was embarrassed and ashamed to have gotten my girlfriend pregnant. I was not raised that way and I felt people would look down on me. It was meant to be that I left that job so I could start fresh and not be ashamed. Looking back, having my son was the best thing that happened to me.

I learned a lot from the different careers that I was in—mostly the art of communication and how to deal with people. I feel that communication is the biggest part of doing business. Being super likable, authentic, and true to what you preach. I am not about ass kissing or making stuff up to gain street cred. Instead, I only talk about and focus on the stuff I am experienced in. Part of my services now is consulting with businesses and helping them grow and expand. I am an ideas guy and I am very good at coming up with creative and strategic ways to implement something new.

From being a nightclub DJ to hunting down fugitives, I am truly lucky to be alive. I always say that I have a guardian angel around me and I feel we all do, but you need to connect with your angel and channel it into your daily life. I have had numerous miracles happen to me, and the only way to explain it is having faith. It is not science or a formula, but rather it is all spiritual and it happens even till this day.

Please follow me on social media, and I would love to know how you liked this book.

Instagram: TheSalonGuy

Twitter: @TheSalonGuy

Facebook: www.facebook.com/TheSalonGuy

YouTube: www.youtube.com/TheSalonGuy

Website: www.thesalonguy.com